The Women's Land Army
and Me

The Women's Land Army
and Me

Marjorie M Dean

The Pentland Press Limited
Edinburgh • Cambridge • Durham • USA

First published in 1995 by
The Pentland Press Ltd.
1 Hutton Close
South Church
Bishop Auckland
Durham

British Library Cataloguing in Publication Data.
A catalogue record for this book is available
from the British Library.

ISBN 1 85821 311 8

Typeset by CBS, Felixstowe, Suffolk
Printed and bound by Antony Rowe Ltd., Chippenham

DEDICATION

This book is dedicated to the love and care given to me by Miss Lilian Brealey, late of Gorman's Terrace, North Tawton, Devon, whom I was proud to call My Auntie Lil. I also thank all those kind landladies who billeted the other land girls. You were the *Salt of the Earth.*

CONTENTS

FOREWORD

The concept to bring young women onto farms was devised during the Great War with Germany, 1914–1918, when the Women's Land Army was first formed in 1917. Britain, being a leading industrial nation, depended heavily on their large Maritime Fleet. These merchant ships brought in cargoes of raw materials as well as a high percentage of food for the table. Fresh food for home consumption was produced by farmers. Because of the high importance of this food supply to Britain, the German Navy mounted a blockade of shipping around the British Isles, using their powerful Navy, surface Raider ships and the highly successful U-Boat submarine fleet.

Many thousands of tons of valuable shipping and their cargoes were sunk, and hundreds of lives were lost. There was no real threat from air attack, as the aeroplane was only in experimental stages at that time, and had a very limited range.

When war again broke out between Britain and Germany in 1939, the blockade of shipping to British ports was again put into place by Germany. By this time, the German fighting fleet had been re-built, improved and upgraded to include the very fast Pocket Battleship, the speedy torpedo boats called E-Boats, and a bigger and more efficient U-Boat submarine fleet. Germany had also developed a large Air Force with a variety of efficient aeroplanes and highly trained pilots and support crews.

Realizing that another blockade of its shipping would severely deplete the food supply, Britain moved quickly to make itself more self-sufficient and less dependent on imported food. They achieved this by stopping the import of luxury foods, introducing rationing of most foods and encouraging home production. From the word go, in 1939, The Women's Land Army was re-formed. This released able-bodied farm-workers to go to the Armed Services, and the resulting 90,000-strong army of women who served as Land Girls were able to increase home food production.

Every member of the Women's Land Army was a volunteer. There was no official call-up for land girls because this very important force was not recognized as a Service Organization. Instead they were treated as poorly paid civilians and were given a uniform to let people see what an important job they were doing. The importance of their job was unquestioned, as everyone had to eat. In their wisdom, the wartime Government treated these girls badly by offering low wages during their service, with no hand-outs on leaving, and no thanks or recognition in later years.

It is not generally accepted that a farm labourer of that period was a very highly skilled person. Much of the work was done by hand in those days, and most farms still used horses to assist with their work. Due mainly to the depression, very few farms had tractors, and farms were graded by the number of horses that they worked. A one-horse farm was small, and a six-horse farm was fairly large. When a land girl replaced a farm labourer, she was expected to become as highly skilled as her predecessor immediately. Some girls became more highly skilled in such jobs as dairy food production, horticulture, animal husbandry and forest management. Most of these jobs would require a university degree today.

The Women's Land Army was disbanded in the early 1950s, but it was not until the early 1990s that it was acknowledged that these girls were 'part of the war effort', and were given recognition by the Ex-Service organizations. But for those of us that do remember what these girls did for us, we offer our lasting thanks and gratitude for the wonderful job that they volunteered for and did so efficiently.

Leslie S Dean
Former Merchant Navy Officer

ACKNOWLEDGEMENTS

- The author wishes to thank Rose, Little Doris and Vi for sending names, details, contacts, help and suggestions to be included in this book. It is much appreciated and adds accuracy to many of the stories.

- To my dear old school friend Mrs Jean Edwards of Dingestowe, Gwent: thank you for wearing those breeches. Without them there would have been no book, no experiences, no lifelong friendships and no happy laughter.

- Sincere thanks and appreciation to Valerie Storen and Karen Pope of Perth, Australia for speedily and accurately transcribing and transposing the mass of material used.

- Finally, I lovingly thank my husband Les, without whose assistance, support, encouragement and drive the project would not have been completed.

CHAPTER 1

JOINING THE WOMEN'S LAND ARMY

It was a lovely afternoon in April 1944 as I made my way home from outer London, where I worked as a post office clerk. Double summer time gave us sunlight till late in the evening in wartime England which seemed to allow us time to get things done before darkness came.

There was a special surprise in store for me this particular day as my old school-friend Jean was home on leave from Wales. I hadn't seen her for months, yet here she was looking so smart and so well in her Women's Land Army uniform. I loved her breeches; they looked terrific. I had no idea that she was in the Land Army. We had so much to talk about, but I could only think of how much I would love to have a pair of breeches like that. She told me about the many jobs she did on the farm and of some of the amusing things that had happened. As I listened, my eyes were fixed on her lovely light brown corduroy breeches. Wouldn't I love a pair of breeches like that! We talked until it was late, and after Jean had gone, I went to bed wishing I had breeches like she had.

Next day at work, my mind kept bringing me back to thoughts about those breeches, so much so that I knew I would have to do something about it. When I got home that night I discussed it with my grandparents who had brought my sister and me up, following the split up of our parents when we were very young. I had never been away from home before, so it was very important for them to agree to me joining the Land Army and leaving home. I was already in what was termed 'a reserved occupation' so there was no need for me to join any of the services. All girls above the age of eighteen who were fit were required to 'join up' in the services or

1

to serve the war effort in munition factories or other war work in reserved occupations.

My grandparents listened carefully and agreed to me joining by saying that they wouldn't stop me from doing what I wanted to do.

I wrote a letter to my boyfriend, Les, and told him that I would be applying to go into the Land Army quite soon. He was away in the Merchant Navy so it could be some time before my letter reached him. We didn't know where the ships were, nor when they would get home as all of these things were TOP SECRET. I then had difficulty in obtaining an application form because of my reserved occupation, but I got around that problem and sent it in. They called me in for an interview to a large office in Central London. This was the furthest I had travelled away from home. I suppose it was the war and the bombing that kept most city people within easy reach of home. There were plenty of buses and trains that were usually full or nearly full. Everyone used public transport as there was no petrol allowed for private travel and most everyday items were rationed.

I was shown into a very large hall where there were a dozen or more ladies at interview tables. These really were *ladies* from the upper class of society, who did this voluntary work to assist the all-over war effort.

All the applicants stood in line and had to go to each table in turn and would be asked questions by each of the ladies. We only spent a few minutes at each table, but I was so keen to be accepted that before I left each lady I asked if I was 'in'. I did this all the way down the line until I came to this dear lady at the far end. She looked at me over the top of her lorgnette spectacles and said, 'My dear, you don't look very strong; you're rather thin, aren't you?' So I said, 'Yes, but I am very wiry.' As I had been interviewed by all of the ladies, I was so enthusiastic to get to know if I was in: I wasn't sure if I had answered their questions properly. So, being told I was rather thin, I thought, 'Dare I ask her if I have passed?'

Then I thought, 'Well, why not?' so I did. She replied, 'I think that you are very enthusiastic and that you will make a lovely land girl.' That made my day.

It's hard to imagine how I felt on my way home. Those few words of encouragement from that dear lady at the end desk had lifted me ten feet off the floor. So when I got home and told them, 'Yes', that I was in, everyone was very pleased: but of course I had to wait for the letter that would confirm this.

My Nan and Granddad said they were very pleased, but I am sure now that they must have had some thoughts about a young girl going miles away in war time. However, they didn't say such things to me, and gave me all the support and co-operation that I needed. The letter of acceptance finally came after what seemed like an eternity. It also said I would be posted to a large house in Devon on a dairying property owned by Wimple the Cider People, and that my uniform would arrive within a day or two.

Arriving at the same time as my letter of acceptance was a letter from my boyfriend saying, 'Please, please whatever you do, don't join the forces.' What was I supposed to do? So I thought, 'Well, it's too late, mate, I've already done it!'

Within a few days the parcel arrived. It was a big parcel and it was welcomed with lots of excitement by all the family. Everyone helped me to open it and they all had to pull out something. Of course there were the breeches. As I pulled them out, I thought, 'This is what started it all off, and here I am holding a pair of breeches that are *mine*!'

There were lots of clothes in the parcel: shirts, a big green pullover, long socks, brown shoes, an overcoat, a hat and all the badges. Then there was the working gear: overalls, big black boots, wellington boots and a long black raincoat and sou'wester hat. After we had sorted it all out, the first thing that I had to put on was the breeches. I thought I really did look good and the family must have done too because there were no bad comments, only good ones. Anyway, no one laughed, but I felt good, and I enjoyed every bit of it.

I often wondered if I made many mistakes during those last few days in the post office where I worked as I was always thinking about what was going to be ahead of me: such questions as 'Will I like it?' 'Who am I going to meet?' and so on. I was just up in the air all the time in anticipation of what was to come. Then, each night as I got home, I just couldn't wait to get out all the gear and try it all on again. The long raincoat, sou'wester and wellington boots made me look like the Black Watch or something. With the hat brim pulled down I was completely hidden from view, and I couldn't see much either.

A few days later I got the letter from headquarters telling me dates, travel information and with the railway pass to my first posting. So at last I was ready to go.

Sitting on the train I wondered how long this journey was going to be. I had no idea as this was my first experience of long-distance travel and there was no family to ask. I was now on my own. But thoughts took over as the miles slipped by. 'Have I done the right thing?'

We did have a lovely happy atmosphere at home. My grandparents were caretakers of a mansion which we occupied almost without interruption for ten years. I was used to all the comforts of such a large house. Lots of rooms to use, three bathrooms, hot water and large grounds surrounding the house. My grandmother was also a dressmaker and she made me lovely clothes to wear. I had packed a few of these although I didn't know if I would have the opportunity to wear them. But then I said to myself, 'The thing is, I am now doing something towards the war effort'. To me that was very important.

In war-time Britain we all had to pull our weight towards the war effort, which everyone did as well as they could. We all felt that we *belonged* and the good feelings and bonds between people were something of which to be proud. You see we *cared* how others got on and shared their problems. Not like today.

CHAPTER 2

MILKING INSTRUCTIONS

When I arrived at my destination and got out at the end of the platform, I realized that I wasn't the only land girl who got off the train. There were four or five other girls who looked as bewildered as I was, so we all headed towards the way out of the railway station in a little group.

Just then a Sergeant-Major type of woman loomed over us and said, 'This way, girls' in an authoritative voice. We then realized that she was the supervisor. She huddled us all into a vehicle which could only be found in the country. It was more like a cart with an engine instead of a horse: but it was better than walking, I suppose. Our thoughts on the ride in this *bone shaker* were swept away by the excitement of being in the country. We arrived at the lovely house and were taken into a nice lunch before being shown into our rooms. There were twelve girls in all who arrived that day to replace twelve girls who had been there for two weeks. There were also twelve girls who had been there one week: they were now called the 'old girls' and we became the 'new girls'.

Each week a dozen new girls turned up to replace the twelve old girls who then were sent out to farms as trained milkmaids. The girls who had been there one week had to show the newcomers what to do. The twelve 'old girls' acted as if they had done farm work for centuries, but in actual fact they had only done it for a week. The new intake of girls started talking to each other and explaining what part of the British Isles they had come from: and they certainly had come from all over, far and wide. I found that many of them were hard to understand, in particular the accents of the girls from Scotland, Wales and the North of England. Also, the people in Devon, where we were, had expressions and an accent that we all found difficult to understand. This caused more laughter than frustration and we all got along very well right from the start.

After tea that night we went up to our room which was a sort of attic, where our iron beds were, and one of the girls said, 'Does anyone want to come and have a look around the village?' This sounded more interesting than staying in, so we all agreed that we might as well go.

We got a feeling of importance as we put our hats on and strutted down to the village. The main street in a Devon village is not filled with the night-life that you would find in the big cities. On a warm night you could sit and watch the world go by, or you could sit and think, if you were energetic.

The main activity was in the village pub where at least some of the locals were actually *moving*. One of the other girls from London said, 'Who's coming in for a drink?' Well, I had never been in a pub for a drink before, but I thought, 'I have joined something new now so I have got to join in with them and their activities.' Inside the low door of the pub were low ceilings and small rooms that could have been there since the world began. It was then that we realized that we were to be addressed as 'M'dear', 'Missie' or 'Maids', if there were more than one of us. They didn't ask, 'Where be yoo'n staying to?' They already knew. Country people notice things if it's someone else's business.

I wasn't used to drinking so I got a small cider, thinking, 'I have got to be careful' as I had heard what drinking can do. The other girls bought different drinks but I wasn't taking much notice of how much they had had. When we got back to the house, which was to be our temporary billet, one of the girls said, 'Oh, I feel sick.' She seemed very young and looked only about seventeen, obviously not used to drinking either. We had to explain that she couldn't go anywhere or she would give the game away. The supervisor couldn't know that, on our first night, we had been into this little pub. We talked her into going to bed.

During the night she kept moaning and groaning and saying, 'I feel sick. Oh, I feel sick'. The only thing I could think of was to put her hat by the side of the bed, and told her, 'If you think you have got to be sick, be sick in that.' I don't think that she realized that it was *her own new hat* that had been placed beside her bed. Luckily, by morning the hat was empty.

Early next morning the supervisor came and gave a heavy knock on all the doors and said, 'Hurry up girls – breakfast time.' We all got out of bed and washed our faces and hands and cleaned our teeth. There was no time for a shower or a bath because there was work to be done on the dairy farm and that is what we had come to learn. We all trotted down the stairs and into the dining room for breakfast.

We were all very excited and didn't really eat much before the supervisor said, 'Right, come along girls, outside.' We were shown into the main yard where all of the cattle had been brought down from the grazing field about a mile and a half up the road. Each cow had been placed into their individual stalls ready for milking. Cows don't really have to be shown where to go because they go to the same stall every day. They had probably been doing it for years. The supervisor then explained that each *new* girl, who had just arrived, would be paired off with one *old* girl, who had been there one week. This was so that the old girls could show the new girls everything that had to be done in milk production, and to get a further week of experience themselves before being posted to individual farms. It was a process where each girl had one week's instruction from an old girl and then one week instructing the next intake of new girls. The supervisor was there to see that everything went smoothly, and told us to take a lot of notice of what the old girls were saying so that we could learn quickly and know exactly what to do.

The girl who had been paired off to teach me showed me into a large sort of wash-house that was scrupulously clean. She told me to take one of the huge pails and to fill it up with hot water and disinfectant. The big pail on its own was quite heavy, but when it was full of hot water you would swear it was stuck to the floor. We also had to take one of the large hand brushes that looked like a *jumbo scrubbing brush*. These certainly weren't designed for dainty work or hands.

To complete our equipment for the job we had to do, we were given a large cleaning cloth each. We took all of this into the yard where the cows were and the supervisor told us what to do. We were told to lift the cow's tail, take hold of the huge brush and brush down the rear end of the cow to get all the hanging bits off. To girls from the city this seemed a bit amusing and there were more than a few giggles as we worked on cleaning up the cows. It was one of those times when a laugh, a chuckle or a giggle helped to put the unpleasant side of the job out of our mind.

Once the brushing was completed to the supervisor's satisfaction, the next job was explained to us: we had to take the cleaning rags and wash under the cow, all over and around the udder and the teats. More giggles and sniggers from the new girls. Then the Cockney girl next to me said, 'I'll wash this one, and you wash the *udder* one.' This time we all burst out laughing because it sounded so funny with a Cockney accent in Devon.

The laughter stopped as quickly as it started when the supervisor shouted, 'Right, simmer down, girls.' She didn't appreciate laughter and wanted us all to get on with the job, so we got on with cleaning the cows ready for milking.

The next job was the milking, and the supervisor showed us into a separate stall where we were introduced to Daisy the cow. Then she explained that Daisy was a very quiet, contented animal that had been chosen for her even temperament, and all the girls were trained on her.

All milking was done by hand in those days and we were all expected to follow the correct procedure, which the supervisor demonstrated to us. First she put a little white hat on her head to keep her hair from falling into the milk. Then she placed a little three legged stool near to the cow's udders. She sat down on the stool and placed a clean pail under Daisy, took hold of two of the diagonal teats at the top, leaned her head on Daisy's body and started milking.

She explained the actions as she went, saying, 'Press and pull, press and pull.' Each time she pulled there was a *swish* as the milk came gushing out into the pail. In a short time the pail was half full and she stopped and said, 'Now who is going to be first to try this?' It looked easy so I said, 'Yes, I'll try that.' So I put on a little cap, sat on the stool and put a clean pail under Daisy. I then took hold of the teats in the correct manner and started to milk, saying to myself, 'Press and pull, press and pull.' But as I said pull, the sound was *ping*. Try again, press and pull and *ping*. I pressed harder, pulled harder and even changed teats, but all I got was one little drip each time. After about a quarter of an hour, all I had got was about an eggcup full of milk.

None of the girls laughed at my miserable effort but perhaps it was because I was first and they hadn't tried yet. Some did do better than I did on the first try, but I thought I would perhaps be better the next day. The next day was not any different. I found hand milking very hard as my wrists used to ache and, no matter how I tried, I didn't seem to improve at all.

Poor old Daisy was a very contented cow as she didn't seem to mind all of us girls pulling her about every day. Maybe she dreaded a new intake of girls every week, but she didn't complain. After watching the other girls try, I could see that some of them were very rough. Thinking back on that now, perhaps you had to be rough to be a good milkmaid.

Wartime advertisement

CHAPTER 3

MILK, COW DUNG AND ME

After a couple of days it was our turn to get the cows in. We were quietly woken about 5 a.m. and got dressed straight away, making as little noise as possible. The supervisor told us not to wake the other girls up and to go quietly down stairs. We had to walk about a mile and a half down the country lane to fetch the cows down.

We set off down the lane at a good brisk pace. The countryside was beautiful early in the morning and we filled our lungs with the clean country air. When we arrived, all the cows were huddled together around the gate waiting to be let down. It was amazing how they knew that it was time to be milked: not one of them had a watch. The girl teaching me was named Annie. She grabbed hold of a huge stick and said to me, 'Get yourself a stick, Marg.' All I picked up was an oversized twig, not very big at all. Annie opened the gate and started hitting the leading cow with her stick as she shouted 'HO! HO!' so that all of Devon could hear. Then she turned to me and said, 'Go on then, this is what you have got to learn.' So I tapped a cow on the backside with my twig and said almost in a whisper 'ho! ho!' The cows didn't really need us to hit them on the bum because they knew exactly what to do, but I suppose it did encourage some of the slower ones to move a bit faster.

We tramped down this country lane and into the big yard. The cows knew exactly where to go and got themselves into their little stalls. As they got into place, Annie and I put the chains around their necks so that they didn't move while they were being milked. After a while all the other girls came out to brush, wash and milk the cows, while Annie and I went inside for a cup of tea and breakfast.

Food didn't seem to worry us for the first few days, but after that the country air and the hard physical work made us ravenous. Several of us from the city had done clerical work before we joined up, but now with farm work and fresh air we felt as if we could eat a horse.

The food was quite good, but I am sure the cooks didn't realize how hungry we girls got. We were never asked if we had had enough to eat, so most evenings we went into the village to buy whatever we could to fill us up. We couldn't buy sweets or chocolate because these luxuries were rationed during the war, and for many years after it ended, so we bought anything that we could eat to fill those empty corners of the stomach.

By the time Annie and I had had our breakfast and returned to the yard, the cows had been milked, so we had to carry on with our allotted job. This was to go into the stalls and unhook the securing chains from each cow's neck. As they were released, each cow walked backwards out of the stall, then turned and walked right through the cowshed into the main yard. This yard was a huge square area that was big enough to hold all of the cows in the herd.

As each cow was released to move out to the main yard, it would lift up its tail and shit all over the place, so the cowsheds and the yard were covered in cow droppings by the time the herd left for the walk back down the lane to the fields, driven by two of the other girls.

The two of us then had to sweep up the mess with *king-sized* brooms, shovel it into a huge wooden barrow and wheel it outside to tip it onto a mountain of cow dung. It seemed as if this dung heap had been there for years. We were both quite slim and found this work very hard and smelly. The brooms and shovels were made with giants in mind and it took all the strength of both of us to get the first barrow-load out to the heap. We made the next barrow-load a bit smaller but it was still very heavy to wheel.

Once the shovelling was completed, we had to hose down the big square yard to clean up the rest of the mess. We had the same job the next day and I thought that there must be an easier way than this to clean up after the cows. I thought about it that day and overnight and had an idea in my head that should make the work easier. As we trotted off down the lane the next morning, I thought about my idea and said to myself, 'Why not?' So on that walk along the lane I briefly outlined my idea of how to make the yard cleaning easier. Annie thought it was a good idea and we decided to try it out. So we opened the gate, let out the cows, shouted HO! HO! a bit louder today, put the chains around the necks of the cows and went to breakfast.

After breakfast, Annie and I returned to the cowshed full of enthusiasm. The cows had been milked and the other girls had left us to do the shitty job of *dung shovelling*. I said to Annie, 'Right, let's get into operation.' The plan was simple enough if we worked together. I went to the cow's head and unhooked the chain. Annie went to the other end and held down the cow's tail so that she couldn't lift it up. She held the tail down firmly as the cow backed out, turned and walked through the cowshed to the yard. At the same time I dashed around through the other door and waited with the shovel. As the cow came out into the yard I held the shovel into position and said to Annie, 'Right, let go.' When she let go, up went the tail and the cow also let go. I had the shovel at about a foot below the cow's bum level. The dollops hit the shovel and splattered all over the place and came all over me.

The first attempt wasn't all that successful but we were having such a good time we decided to try again on the second one. No need to tell you that the same thing happened, except that as Annie came into the yard with the cow, and as I called out 'Let go' this cow wasn't satisfied with lifting its tail and doing it all over me: she kept walking out into the yard, so I had no alternative but to follow the cow's behind and to try to catch it as she was doing it.

Although my idea wasn't really working, Annie and I were laughing and having such a good time, that no one would ever guess that we were doing something to help the war effort. Really we were only trying to save ourselves a lot of work. The next few cows did the same thing and kept walking. None of them wanted to just stand still so that I could catch it on the shovel and drop it into the barrow that Annie was now pushing alongside of me. The barrow was necessary because of the amount of shit that came from each cow. It took more than one shovel-full to catch it. We were having such a good time and kept trying. We thought that no one was worrying about us as no one was looking.

Then a voice bellowed from nowhere, 'What do you think you're doing, girls!' Yes, it was the supervisor. She came over to us and said, 'My God! Never have I seen anything like this before!'

Poor old Annie and I just stood with our heads down and chose to say nothing. My thoughts told me that this supervisor had no sense of humour whatsoever as she didn't even grin. We must have looked funny, particularly me because I was by now covered in shit: it was all over my clothes, hands and my face and hair. I must have smelt lovely too.

We were ordered in to wash ourselves, change our clothes then come back and do the job properly. After our clean-up, it was back to the stalls to do the usual thing. Well, we had tried to use our initiative hadn't we?

There were still chuckles from Annie and me as we went about our work that day. But later that afternoon the supervisor came over to us and said, 'Come along, you two girls, I have a job for you.' As we followed her, she said, 'If you think that mucking about with cow's dung is fun, come and see if you enjoy this.' She opened a large barn which had cow dung that was about a foot deep and well trodden down. It looked and felt as hard as cement. We were given two shovels and told to dig that out. After she left, we got stuck into digging out years of hard cow dung.

Although we worked solidly and hard, we didn't manage to finish it all. I suppose that was the punishment that she wanted to lash out at us. It didn't really spoil our day because we were still laughing at ourselves and how we looked to each other.

That night we were the main story-tellers as the other girls listened to what had happened. They all thought it must have been hilarious but no one else was game to try it. Maybe they didn't want to get the same punishment as we had. A group of girls seem to have fun listening to an incident like this and many of them threw in little comments to add to the humour. One even came up with a name for a supervisor with no sense of humour, but that is unprintable.

Needless to say, Annie and I were given an extra day on the early morning call to bring in the cows, and of course to shovel and clean up the yard. So off we went, brought down the cows, tied them up and went in for breakfast. We agreed that there would be no bright new ideas used today.

As we returned to the yard there was a big commotion going on. We had missed something that had happened while we were eating, so we asked what was going on. One of the other girls told us that they had lost the bull. Most city girls wouldn't notice that there was a lot of difference between a bull and a cow.

Once they had found him and sorted everything out, they found that I had tied up the bull to be milked. It wasn't long before the supervisor loomed over me again and said, 'How on earth could you tie a bull up to be milked?' It was better not to answer, but I thought, 'Well it didn't seem difficult to me.'

Next day, Annie and I didn't have to bring the cows down and were told to get back to milking. I sometimes wonder if they thought that we were not suited to shouting 'HO! HO!' The reason for me being at the Training Centre was to train as a milkmaid to go out onto a farm after the two weeks' training. However, I persevered with the hand milking but I still didn't master the art. It didn't matter how hard I tried, I didn't progress beyond, 'Press, pull and PING'. And two eggcups full seemed to be my best effort. Each evening my wrists ached so much, through trying so hard and so long. When I told the supervisor that I found it very difficult she said she did understand. It was nice to see that she wasn't nasty all the time.

The next morning she came to me and said, 'If you are finding it hard to do milking, perhaps you should think of something different that you can do in the Land Army.'

This was interesting so I asked, 'What other job can I try?' She then said, 'Have you thought of going on gang work?' I didn't know what this was and she explained that there were groups of approximately twelve land girls that formed a gang to do general farming work. These gangs went to different farms as they were needed and were usually under the control of an Agricultural Committee. There was one not far away in Devon.

After thinking about my situation, I realized that I could probably be more suited to gang work. I liked the country work that had been associated with a dairy farm but I knew now that a milkmaid I would never be. Once again, the supervisor was sympathetic when I said I would like to try gang work. Even though I had been in her bad books a couple of times, she must have realized how keen I was to do well.

After a couple of days, the supervisor told me I had been given a position in North Tawton in Devon. It wasn't far away and I was to leave the next day. I found it very difficult saying cheerio to the girls whom I had known just over a week and I'm sure that several of them wished that they were coming with me. The next job was a new challenge that I was looking forward to.

CHAPTER 4

THOUGHTS ON THE TRAIN

A s I sat on the train going to North Tawton, I thought about home. I had spent ten years in Shrewsbury House where my grandfather was the caretaker for the Woolwich Borough Council. The Council had purchased this mansion to house a library and museum for the ratepayers and residents of Shooters Hill and surrounding districts. Standing in one acre of land, the house was built in 1924 for the second wife of a wealthy builder. No cost had been spared for materials and fittings. Entry was by double wrought-iron gates, hanging on large ornamental square pillars with a matching pedestrian gate to one side. The drive entered the courtyard at the front of an impressive three-storey mansion. There was a large, covered main entrance on ornate pillars with a balcony above. Inside, rooms were very large with extensive use of oak panelling, highly polished floors and ornate ceilings, extravagant wooden staircases and bannisters. The museum did not eventuate, but the library opened in 1938. Much to Granddad's disgust.

A carpet strip down the centre of the hallway led to the library room, to keep marks off the highly polished floors each side. Large pictures hanging on the walls gave it an arty look. Sadly, people, and especially children, would stand on the polished floor to get a closer look at these pictures, leaving dusty footprints and Blanco from their clean white shoes. This brought out the worst attitude in Granddad who kept those polished floors looking like glass. For, after all, it was *his* house.

On the outbreak of war in 1939, the house was sandbagged and internally shored to become an Air Raid Control Centre on the ground floor with

Shewsbury House: front entrance

Shrewsbury House: rear view

control room, map room, telephone room and staff dining room and amenities. The first floor housed the Town Clerk and other dignitaries. We were then confined to the five rooms of the top floor for our accommodation during the war period.

Jobs were hard to get before the war but, when I was fourteen, Nan got me a job working as an apprentice photographer at 'Tasma Studios', a high-class photographic business much in demand for society weddings, children's portraits and for military photographs for high-ranking army officers, cadets and graduates of the military college. Many memories of this job come to mind: those of many hours in the dark room, hands in cold water to develop film, long working hours and a 1^d Fyfes banana for lunch still remain. But I was very happy in my job with $7/6^d$ a week wage. Sweeping the front of the shop was a job I didn't enjoy, but serving the customers with photographic and art supplies was a real pleasure. Being brought up by my grandparents, I knew a Victorian standard of etiquette and behaviour. Each day as I set off for work, my Nan would usually remind me by saying, 'Be polite to customers and greet them with a smile.'

Dusting stock shelves and photograph frames was one of my many other jobs. I became quite proficient with a big feather duster while waiting for customers (I still dislike dusting to this day!) Being young, very innocent, quietly reserved, and naïve, I had to learn the correct way to deal with customers. Having been brought up by grandparents, I found no difficulty in talking to older people.

I recall one day I had put down my feather duster to serve a high-ranking Army Officer who had called to collect portraits of himself which weren't quite ready. I didn't know his rank but he was very high up and what they called a 'red tab' officer. He was a real gentleman with a cultured Oxford accent. As he walked and looked around the shop, he said, 'It's cold today, isn't it, Miss?' As I answered, he sort of half-spluttered and half-choked and just then the owner came out with his framed photograph and he left.

Sitting at the table that night I told Nan and Granddad that I had talked to a high Army Officer that day. Of course they asked what he had said and I told them that he said, 'Cold today, isn't it, Miss?' and that I had replied, 'Yes, Sir, it's cold enough to freeze the balls off a brass monkey.' Granddad burst out laughing, but Nan exploded. 'I told you, Dad, not to say things like that in front of these girls! Now see what it's done!' I had no idea then that what I had said was barrack-room talk. Wonder what the General said when he got back.

It wasn't long before the German air force started bombing raids on London. With superior air power they were able to bomb in the daytime as well as at night. All we could do to help our depleted air force was to help the Spitfire Fund and shake our fists as the Gerry planes went over. For me to walk to and from work in an air raid was too dangerous, so I left the photographer's when Nan got me a job inside Shrewsbury House on the Air Raid Control Staff.

I was a junior in the map room where each 'incident' was reported, plotted and action initiated. Air Raid Wardens reported a bomb or incendiary drop or some other 'incident', such as a plane crash, to Control, and we would call out fire, ambulance, police, bomb disposal, heavy and light rescue or whatever service was needed. This ensured repair for gas, water, electricity and telephone services.

The operation of saving life, rescue and repair was co-ordinated from this control. We also advised on unsafe roads to be avoided by emergency services. This work was very different to photography and art: however, it was very interesting. The hours worked were also different as we worked in three shifts of 24 hours on duty with 48 hours off. This ensured that Air Raid Control was continuous 24 hours a day, seven days a week, the roster system giving a fair distribution of Sunday work to everyone.

My Nan became the cook for meals in the canteen and Granddad continued as caretaker but also sat inside the main door to check everyone who came to the building, as entry was controlled. Also waiting inside the door were the messengers: young boys who rode bikes to take messages by hand to the Town Hall and various other places where an urgent delivery was required.

The war they said would only take six months had been on a year and didn't look like ending. It was September 1940, I was sixteen, and a new messenger boy had just started out front. He got on well with Granddad and they talked a lot while on the door. He told Granddad that his name was Les, he was sixteen and had been evacuated from London to Somerset to finish a three-year navigational course. He was about to join his first ship as an apprentice officer but it had been bombed in London docks, so he now had to wait for another one. The merchant-shipping companies were reluctant to take on young apprentices because the sea in wartime was so dangerous.

As the staff passed through the entrance hall to the canteen several times a day, Granddad noticed that Les seemed excited about one of the girls. Les said to Granddad, 'The one in the green cardigan looks very nice.' Granddad said, 'Oh, she is. The best one in the house.' To which Les added, 'Do you think I could take her to the pictures?' 'You had better ask her,' said Granddad. 'She does look very nice,' Les continued. 'Yes,' said Granddad with a twinkle in his eye as he stroked his moustache with the back of his hand, 'She's my Granddaughter you know!' Yes, they were talking about me. Nan said I should raise my hat to the new messenger. He seemed very young but we did go to the pictures and got on very well together.

One December day Nan told me to get my best clothes on as there was someone special coming to tea at 5.30. When I asked, 'Who?' she said, 'Wait and see.' At 5.30 there were footsteps on the stairs. When I looked over it was someone in naval uniform, probably for the Town Clerk. The footsteps kept coming then on to the stairs to the top floor. I looked again. It was Les in his merchant-navy uniform. I was so surprised I said, 'Whose uniform have you got on?' and with a big smile he simply said, 'It's mine.' Nan was matchmaking and gave us tea alone together, set out on an oval, barley-twist, gate-leg table. It was a memorable night that we still celebrate. I spilled tea over Les's uniform and he kissed me for the first time. To this day our prize possession is that gate-leg table and 1st December at 5 minutes to 7 is a *special anniversary*.

A vacancy came in the map-room staff and Les got transferred to the same shift as me. One evening there were just three of us in the map room:

Mr Turnbull, who pretended to be asleep, Les and me. Mr Turnbull was a bachelor about late 40s who made out he was sleeping to hear what we said to each other. We didn't say or do anything out of place but he must have got a kick out of it somewhere. Just then the emergency 999 phone rang. Les answered: 'My wife's water's burst,' said the voice. Les took the name and address and said he would send someone right away. He made a phone call, gave the address and told them the problem, wrote out the 'incident' form with action taken duly completed and passed it through to the control room. The controller rushed about a bit but said nothing. You see Les was as naïve as I was: he did not send the ambulance, he sent the *water board*. I bet they didn't find the stopcock.

CHAPTER 5

ARRIVING AT NORTH TAWTON

N orth Tawton railway station was much the same as any station for a country village in the West Country: a platform, a seat and a small shelter for waiting passengers, all of which was enclosed by a paling fence. This formed a type of security for law-abiding people. A small goods office near a space on the end of the platform was used for the supplies for the village which came by train, and for produce that was sent by train to the market towns. Not all passenger and goods trains stopped at the station.

As we pulled into the station I took my case from the luggage rack, opened the carriage door and stepped onto the platform. I was met by a very nice lady called Mrs Phillip. She was the Land Army Welfare Officer for the district, who took care of billeting and the general well-being of all land girls in the area. We walked a little further along the platform to meet another girl who was also on the train, and had been sent to North Tawton to join the gang workers.

Mrs Phillip had a wartime petrol allowance for her car so she drove us from the station to the village. It was quite a long way to the village along country lanes and the countryside looked as beautiful as the pictures on a postcard. The village of North Tawton was a lovely place with its rows of small cottages, tiny pubs and delightfully quaint shops and post office. The village square had a tall and majestic clock tower as its centrepiece, with the old Town Hall, larger houses and shops surrounding it. A short way down the road to the right was an ornate archway and gate that took you through to a stone church complete with spire, weather vane and churchyard. Time doesn't ever seem to change the small country village and this one was no exception.

We took the road to the left of the clock tower and the car slowed down at a little lane just down the hill from the square. We turned into this lane where there was a row of little cottages that looked like a small train, and it was in one of these cottages where I was to be billeted. These cottages were probably several hundred years old but still looked very solid. They looked small with low doors and small windows, but had a very tidy appearance with little gardens and a single scrubbed step at each front door.

Mrs Phillip knocked at one of the little doors and introduced me to the lovely, gentle-looking lady who opened it. This was to be my landlady whom I was to call Auntie Lil. She was not very tall, immaculately clean and had a wise-looking, gentle face and a warm smile. She said, 'Come in, m'dear,' in a soft rich Devon accent. As Mrs Phillip left to place the other girl into a billet a short way away, I stepped into this lovely little cottage that was to be my home. After living in a mansion for all those years, then going to the big house at the dairy farm, a country cottage looked very small; but once I had taken in the low ceiling and small rooms, the one thing that impressed me was how clean and tidy this cottage was. Then I was shown through the cottage and was asked if I would like to see my room. Through the hallway to a back room were the stairs to the bedroom. Auntie led the way up to a dear little bedroom with a double bed, a wardrobe, a chair and a washstand and basin. The room, the sheets, the bed, curtains and windows were all beautifully clean. Auntie said, 'There you are, m'dear, this is your room that you will be sharing with another girl called Vi.' She would be home from work a little later on.

Auntie said that I would like Vi because she was a very nice girl. She then said, 'You come downstairs and we will have a nice cup of tea, a little chat and get to know one another.'

We went downstairs to the back room, through the little passage and into the front room. This was the main living room that was used for just about every daytime activity. It was a sitting room, a dining room and even used for cooking so it was always warm and cosy. When there is a

The Square, North Tawton

fireplace in a room it usually becomes the focal point, especially on cold days.

Set in a fireplace with a mantelpiece and valance, there was a cast iron stove with hob plates and oven, with the fire-box to one side. It was an old design but made so that kettle and saucepans could heat up on the top, with baking done in the oven. There was a door in front of the fire-box which held the heat inside the stove for cooking when closed and heated the room when opened. With the door open you could see the red-hot coals and flames of the fire through front grating bars. These fires were cleaned with *Zebo* black grate polish and made to shine with a soft flat brush with a handle on the top. This grate was always cleaned and polished to a deep shining black, which contrasted the beautiful white starched doilies placed under vases and ornaments. The whole room was enhanced by the net, floral, draw curtains over the crisp, white lace curtains to the window. It was all so compact, cosy and comfortable.

The kettle was already hot and soon boiled over the hob on the stove, so the tea was quickly made and allowed to draw while we talked. Auntie didn't ask many questions really, but I was made to feel at home immediately. She was so easy to talk to and there was something special about country tea made with rainwater boiled over a fire.

As we chatted and drank our tea, there was probably a thousand things that someone as houseproud as Auntie was had to do, but she didn't hurry and seemed to enjoy our conversation, as much as I did.

Just then Violet came in and Auntie said, 'Ah there we are, Vi, come in and meet our new little girl.' As Violet came in I thought what a lovely girl she was; we said hello and then she went upstairs to wash and when she came down we had a lot to ask and plenty to talk about: where I had come from, where I had been and, of course, I asked about the gang work. We were both at ease and comfortable with each other's company.

Then Auntie said, 'Come along, girlies, the dinner is ready,' and there was this beautiful meal: a roast with four vegetables and gravy. I must have eaten like a horse because by then I was so hungry; probably a hunger that had accumulated over the hard days at the dairy farm. Then, to top it all off after that delicious dinner, we had some beautiful afters. This was the first time that I had had afters since I left home. Again, I showed my appreciation by eating it all. There was no doubt in my mind that we must keep this very secret: our Auntie was the best landlady, the best cook with the best food and I had been lucky enough to be chosen to be billeted there.

After dinner we sat around the fire talking. We all had so much to talk about but we had to go to work the next day, so it was suggested that we go to bed. Auntie said, 'Just a minute, girlies, let's have a cup of cocoa.' After a nice warm drink we went up to bed. Vi and I had got along famously. We were at ease with each other and kept chatting as we went upstairs in the dark. Once we were in our room at the top of the stairs, Vi lit a candle. I said, 'Why are you lighting a candle? There's electric light here.' Vi replied, 'We are not allowed to use electricity because Auntie says it's too dear.' That didn't worry me so we got undressed and got into bed. We carried on talking, a lot quieter than before, the mellow flame of the candle moving to every little breeze that hit it. I thought how relaxing the candlelight was as we talked. We said goodnight, blew out the candle and went to sleep.

The next morning we were woken up by Auntie who had brought us a cup of tea as she said, 'Good morning, girlies, lovely day.' We drank our tea, got out of bed and went over to the old-fashioned water jug and basin that was on the washstand. As Vi poured the water from the jug into the basin I said, 'Shall I go down and get some hot water?' To my surprise Vi replied, 'Oh no, you don't wash in hot water, you wash in cold.'

Country cottage life was full of surprises. An outside toilet, cooking on the fire, candlelight and cold-water washes. Well, I thought, if that is usual practice I had better get used to it. I was wide awake after washing myself in cold water. We got dressed in our working clothes, came down the stairs and into the little sitting room. There on the table was the most beautiful breakfast of bacon and eggs. How ever did she do it with food so short in wartime? This was accompanied by Auntie's daily favourite of fried potatoes and fried vegetables left over from the day before. I learned later that we were to get a huge breakfast like this every day. Country-life surprises were not all that bad were they?

After breakfast it was time to go to work and Auntie gave us each a tin with our lunch in and a flask of tea. As we stepped outside, we were met by two other girls who were billeted next door. Vi introduced them as Rose from London and Pauline from the North of England. They seemed nice girls; both blonde and very cheerful.

We all chatted together as we trotted up towards the clock tower where we were to join our transport. At the clock tower, when we arrived, there stood an old baker's delivery van. The rear part was covered and we entered at the back which was open except for a tail-board. This tail-board was fixed and did not open, and we had to climb aboard up a little ladder that was slung out from inside. Seats were arranged in a U shape with the open end of the U at the back, where I was given a seat. The van wasn't full when we all climbed in but all of the girls whom I had met seemed very nice. Then along came an auburn-haired girl and one of the girls in the van said, 'Come on, Hilda, we are all here.' Hilda was the only one there who could drive. She got in, started up the van and off we went to the next village to pick up Jack.

On the way I learned that Jack was the foreman of our gang; a man about 40, the girls thought. At the next village, Sampford Courtenay, Jack was already outside his cottage. He had a pleasant, bright-red face and not a tooth in his head. To us girls of around 20, he was an old man. He greeted us all with 'Good morning, maids,' climbed up the ladder and clambered over the back, helped by all the girls. He said hello to me in a form of welcome, and could probably see that I was at ease and fitted in well with the other girls. 'He must be all right to work for,' I thought, as he wasn't carrying a whip.

Two more girls were picked up further down the road in the same village and to add to the name puzzle they were both called Rose. The gang was now complete and we set off to the day's job.

CHAPTER 6

SLINGERS

We drove through the country lanes, for what seemed like a long way, to a farm. The job can only be described as general clearing which seemed to come very easy to me. The morning slipped by quite quickly as I got to know the other girls. This was great. It suited me much better than the wrist-aching job of milking a cow, and I really enjoyed the company and the fun and laughter, as they made light work of every job we did.

When lunchtime came I was again ready to eat despite having had that huge breakfast. Although I was very slim, I still managed to burn up a lot of energy working in the country and looked forward to my food.

We all clambered back into the van and sat in the same positions that we had occupied that morning. I took up my place at the end as before and we all opened our lunch tins. As it was the first time I had opened my tin, I was highly delighted to see a beautiful Cornish pasty. A pasty was made with potatoes, turnips, swedes and other cooked vegetables that were chopped up small and placed inside a pastry casing. The pastry had a fancy pattern where it was joined, and it came out a light golden brown when it was baked. This one was big and I took it out of the tin, held it with both hands, and took a bite. It was beautiful and, as I chewed each bite, it was obvious that I was really enjoying the lovely flavour.

It was quiet in the van as I chewed away and when I looked around, I saw that the other girls were staring at me. They didn't say anything but I had to wonder what was happening. I carried on eating as each of them took something out of their tin. I continued to enjoy the tasty cooking of my Auntie when I noticed something whiz past my eyes. A few seconds later there was another whizzing past me. Then I realized that they were throwing food out of the back of the van. With food so short this seemed terrible, but it was my first day and I didn't want to say anything to upset them. So I kept my thoughts to myself. Then one of the girls said, 'Don't worry about that Marg, you're eating yours.' But when I asked, 'Why?' she said, 'Would you like mine?' Of course I said, 'Yes, please.' Then another girl said, 'Would you like mine?' to which I replied, 'Thank you very much.' In the end, most of the girls handed their pasties to me. No need to say that I couldn't possibly eat them all, so I said 'Well I'll save these.' Then they all started laughing so I had to ask why.

Little Doris explained that they were not pasties: 'We call them Slingers.' Once again I asked, 'Why?' and she said, 'Well we just sling them out every day.' When I heard this I couldn't keep my thoughts to myself any longer and said, 'What, and throw these away?' For my benefit, they explained that they all got pasties for lunch every day, and that they were fed up with them. I told them that I would never get fed up with them. Later I learned that a pasty was a good meal that could be

1944 Slinger break while stooking
Big Doris, Birdie, Nobby, Marg, Pauline, Vi, Joan, Rose, Brenda

made cheaply, and that each of the girls' Aunties baked a whole week's supply of pasties every Sunday morning. As I sat there, I was now holding more than one week's supply of pasties, that of course I couldn't eat. I had to reassure the girls that I wouldn't say anything to my Auntie or any of the others that Sunday morning's pasty-bake went out the back of the van. And do you know what? It wasn't long before I was also calling them Slingers, as I slung my pasty out the back of the van without a care; and Slingers is the name I have continued to use all my life when ever I see a pasty. No need to tell you that I didn't say a thing to anyone about the terrible waste of food as none of us would say anything to upset our Aunties.

Funny how all the visitors to North Tawton noticed how well fed the birds, bunnies and other wildlife were. Only the Land Army girls from our gang knew why.

Back at work in the afternoon it was just as pleasant as the morning had been. Knock-off time was 5 o'clock on this sort of work and it seemed to come quickly. We packed up our tools, and all got into our places in the van. The ride back to the village didn't seem so far. We all talked and laughed freely as the girls got to know me.

When we got to the bottom of the hill where we lived, Hilda pulled into the garage. Several of the girls got out and went into the shop where Joe, the owner, allowed them to buy their cigarettes on tick. Sort of 'Smoke now and pay later'. Cigarettes were supplied by Joe all the week, and the accounts were settled up when we were paid every Friday. I didn't smoke then, and felt as if I was the odd one out. At that time it was very fashionable to smoke: smokers used to say that it calmed their nerves. They would justify the bad habit by saying that their name could be on the next bomb, so they should enjoy it while they could. Putting cigarettes on the slate became a vicious circle: when the girls paid up each Friday, all of their money was gone and they started the slate again. All of the girls were reliable and paid up, so Joe was happy.

Once back home, Vi and I had a wash (country style). Very soon there was another lovely dinner on the table just as good as the night before, followed by a beautiful afters. Despite the Slingers incident, I ate everything that was put before me. After dinner, Vi said, 'How about coming up to our club, Marg?' She told me that the land girls had a little club room in the village where we could talk, write letters, play records and have a cup of tea. It was in a shop that had been vacated by a butcher, which had then been taken over by the Women's Voluntary Services: WVS as they were known. It was the WVS ladies who had given us permission to use the facility as our club.

After dinner we went upstairs to change out of our working clothes. It's hard to imagine now how we undressed to our bras and knickers, and had a wash down in cold water. I can only think that we kept warm by moving much faster than we do now. We put on civvy dresses and brushed our hair.

The club was exclusive to our gang of land girls but we could invite visitors. Being a working day, there would only be a few of the girls there, but it was normal behaviour to go properly dressed. In fact, it was second nature to dress tidily when ever we went out. I kept with Vi as we trotted up the hill, and she showed me the way to the club.

The door was open because a couple of the girls were already there. I looked around and saw a medium-sized room containing upright chairs, a table, blackout curtains at the windows, with some pictures and a calendar on the walls. There was also a low cupboard containing cups, saucers and tea-making facilities on top, and a wind-up gramophone with a stack of 78 records. Some of the older records had been donated by the local people, but the new records had been bought from the club funds donated each week by the land girls. They had bought a record a week out of their funds and each girl had a turn to go and choose a new one. It was a pleasant evening and I was to spend many happy hours in the club in the months to come.

We weren't late getting back home as it was back to work next day. Once again, Auntie made us a cup of cocoa before bed. It was while I was drinking mine that I noticed that Auntie drank half a cup of her cocoa, then filled it up with hot water from the kettle. At first I thought her cocoa was too strong, but when she filled it up the second and third time I knew that couldn't be right. With so many refills of hot water, it must have been pretty thin towards the bottom. I suppose it was one of her great pleasures and she didn't want it to come to an end.

I took to gang work like a duck takes to water. It didn't take me very long to realize that, even if I had mastered hand milking, the job was repetitive and must be very boring, whereas this work was different almost every day. We went to many farms in the district which meant we met different people and, although farm work follows a yearly cycle, we did get such a variety of work to do. Some jobs were hard, heavy, back breaking or rough on the hands and feet, but others were a real breeze and we were able to relax a little. When the work was heavy or hard, we all prayed for rain or bad weather so that we could have a rest. The sight of a black cloud or the sound of a thunderstorm brought big smiles to faces and shouts of joy to our lips. When heavy rain came, a crowd at a football match couldn't cheer as loud as the twelve girls of the North Tawton gang.

One of the routine jobs we did during my first few weeks was hedging and ditching. We had to cut back the new growth in the hedges or train the runners to grow over any gaps. New saplings that had sprung up in the wrong place were chopped down with a sharp axe. The hedges formed fences to the fields and were provided by nature. Ditches carried water off the fields and roadways and had to be cleaned out: weeds and stinging nettles would overgrow them and stop them up. We seemed to find humour in most jobs we did. On one occasion I was working in a ditch with several of the girls. We were spaced out every ten feet, slashing weeds and nettles with bill hooks. The other half of the gang were above us doing hedging. Rose was in charge of an axe that day, and we heard the solid sound as the axe hit wood with several heavy blows. Then Rose stood back and bellowed 'TIMBER!' We all scrambled out of the ditch as quickly as we could. Poor old Pauline slipped over and put her hand on the stinging nettles and a couple of us pulled her out of the ditch. We didn't hear the tree fall, but luckily it hadn't fallen our way. When we looked at the ground by Rose's feet, all she had chopped down was a sapling about six feet tall and two inches in diameter. One of the girls who had scrambled out of the ditch with me said, 'Oh, Rose, if you had asked me I could have kicked that tree out with my boot,' and I think she probably could have done. From then on, every sapling, large or small, was dropped to the yell of 'TIMBER!'

CHAPTER 7

FROM HARVESTING TO HIGH SOCIETY

We worked from 8 a.m. to 5 p.m. Monday to Friday and 8 a.m. to 12 noon on Saturdays. There were times during harvesting and haymaking when we had to work longer because we only had the machines for a set number of days, but this was not very often.

Saturday afternoons held a special treat for Vi and me. This was the afternoon that we went to the big house on the Square directly opposite the Town Hall. The house was owned by village dignitaries who we believed were rich farmers. It was a lovely house and big by country standards; however, it wasn't anywhere near as big as the mansion where I came from. Our treat was that we were allowed to use the bathroom in the house to have a *bath*. Each Saturday we walked up the hill with our soap, towel and clean undies in a brown paper bag, knocked on the door, and were taken to the bathroom. We had to be quick as we were only allowed about half an hour to bath and wash our hair. It was so different to being at home where I used to lay in a bath of hot water with only my head sticking out; I could soak for as long as I liked and kept topping up with more hot water as it cooled off; as the hot water came in at the plughole end, I would sit up and swish it up the other end with my hands, then lay down to soak again. However, our Saturday bath was total luxury compared to a wash down in cold water.

Our hair would still be damp when we got back to Auntie's and we would curl it up with pipe cleaners. These were made of soft wire and covered in a fluffy material; they would stay in any shape that they were twisted to. In those days, a ladies' hairdresser was for those who had a lot

34

more money than we did. Once our hair was curled up in pipe cleaners, we covered it with a scarf tied in a turban until it dried. After tea we would get changed into our finery and get ready to go out.

Most Saturdays there would be a dance at the Town Hall, and people came from far and wide to be there. This also included many of the servicemen of the Allied Forces who were stationed in the area. Music was provided by a local band led by Charlie Bissett. Most of the time the band consisted of piano, drums and saxophone but some weeks there were four, when a chap with a cornet joined them. Charlie Bissett was a farm labourer and it looked as if all he did to get ready to play was to wash his hands and face, or just his hands if he was running late, otherwise he looked as if he had come straight in from the farm work.

We often sang as we went along in the van to the tune of *MacNamara's Band*, but our words went like this:

> My name is Charlie Bissett
> I'm the leader of the band
> And though we're small in number
> We're the best in all the land,
> Hennesy, Tennesy, toot the flute,
> The music's really grand,
> The best band in North Tawton is
> Charlie Bissett's band.

Our singing advertisement must have paid off because they booked him every week. The dances were great fun where we met a lot of people. Some of the service personnel were smashing dancers. The other girls and I never had to sit-out a dance, unless we chose to. Most of us had lovely dresses that were the envy of the local girls. Maybe the locals could have matched our dress sense if they had tried, but there is no way that they could have matched our style.

Sunday was a day of rest for us. After a week of gang work followed by the Saturday night dance we deserved to put our feet up. So on Sunday mornings our Auntie always gave us her own secret treat: this was to bring us our breakfast in bed because, as she put it, 'You girlies have to work so hard.' We were given a tray with a boiled egg each, toast, butter and a cup of tea. We could not tell anyone about that, Auntie told us. Then came the big secret! She followed up with scones, jam and *thick cream.* Now, even in the country, cream was very scarce, extremely hard to get, and was a total luxury, and here was Vi and me living it up better than the Ritz. How Auntie managed to get hold of something as difficult as cream still remains a mystery to me. Of course, we were sworn to secrecy and told that we were to tell *no one*, not even the other girls. I had always been able to keep any secret and never tell, and Vi did the same. It kept the supply up, and allowed us to continue a wonderful lifestyle, to which we wanted to become accustomed. This secret treat continued right up to the last Sunday before we left the Land Army, and none of the other girls ever knew.

One of the hardest jobs was the harvesting because we had to work at the same pace as the harvester. There could be no time for slacking off or going slow. Farming methods were very different then: there was so much of the work that had to be done by hand, before, during and after the harvester had operated. When the corn was ripe, it was cut by the reaping machine and bound into heavy bundles called sheaves. Our first job was to follow this machine and pick up the sheaves. Several of these sheaves were stood up in the field into a pyramid arrangement called a stook. The ear part of the corn was placed upper-most to finish drying off. When we had a shower of rain overnight, the sheaves had to be re-stooked to get them thoroughly dry. The sheaves could not be stacked until this drying had been satisfactorily completed. The drying was done naturally by the sun and wind, the same as washing drying on a clothes line.

We were called back to one farm to re-stook as there had been rain overnight. Stooks were being rearranged to assist the drying process, bringing the damp corn to the outside. We were all working away quite steadily, as we didn't have to keep pace with a machine this time. Suddenly, one of the girls, called Brenda, started jumping, throwing her arms in the

1944 Ready for work

Nobby, Rose, Birdie, Vi, Lt Doris, Hilda, Pauline, Joan, Rosie, Marg, Big Doris. In front: Brenda

air and screaming. Several of us said, 'What's wrong with you? What's wrong with you?' But all she could say was, 'There's a mouse. There's a mouse,' then hastily added, 'Quick, quick do something!' A quick reply asked, 'What can we do? What can we do?' with some urgency. Poor Brenda continued to wave her arms and scream out for help. I said, 'We've got to do something, she looks as if she's going hysterical.' The only thing I knew was to slap her face, so I told the girls. They said, 'You slap her face,' meaning me. So I said, 'No, I'm not going to, because she's got a bit of a temper.' By this time Brenda was really distressed and upset. As she screamed out and cried, she was feeling all around her trouser legs and waist. Finally Nobby said, 'Someone has got to do something,' so we all said, 'Well, you do it.' Nobby said to Brenda, 'Right, where is it?' and the reply was, 'Down here, down here.' Nobby thrust her hand in Brenda's dungarees and felt around till she located the mouse, grabbed it and pulled it out.

When we all saw the mouse we all started screaming, dancing and waving our arms about. Nobby wasn't happy either because she was still holding the mouse and wasn't sure what to do with it. Finally, she threw it as far away from us all as she could. We all quietened down to recover from a terrifying experience. Then we went over to Brenda to pacify her and to say how sorry we were that it took us so long to help her.

As we all slowly simmered down we decided to take steps to prevent such a thing happening again. There was still a lot of re-stooking to do and mice were sheltering under quite a few of the pyramids. Most of us took the double precaution of tucking our dungarees into our socks and tying string around the legs below the knees. The twelve of us had been terrified when Nobby held that mouse. The mouse didn't appear concerned, but I bet that his little knees were knocking.

When the corn was dry, we had to bring in the sheaves and stack them. This was a big job and the weather didn't always look too kind, but it stayed fine. We had extra help to bring in and stack the corn. Once the sheaves were all stacked, a thatch was put over the top of them to keep them safe until we started the threshing.I had no idea what was meant by the name threshing. Naughty little boys at school were *thrashed*, but I was soon to find out that it wasn't a bit like that.

Most nights the girls were to go to our club room for company. Even though we worked all day together, we got on extremely well and had an empathy that bonded us together. We got to know each other fairly well, and were able to talk about things that we wouldn't mention to the village people. Much of our time was spent listening to music and having a smoke and a cup of tea. If one girl was energetic, or wanted to put on a particular record, she would go to the gramophone, wind it up and put the music on. These old gramophones were good but you had to work for them. The music was scratchy if you didn't change the needle every few records. If it wasn't wound up enough, the music got slower and lower, or if it was set to more than 78 revolutions a minute, the music was played too high and too fast.

Being so close to one another it wasn't difficult to see when one of the girls was upset, homesick or just out of sorts. The only contact we had with our families and boyfriends was by post. Sometimes these letters contained news of an event we would have liked to have attended, or bad news that we didn't want to read. At that time you either kept it to yourself, shared it with one of the girls or told them all the good or bad news.

When one of the girls was upset, we would all try to cheer her up by talking about it or talking about something else. Music always played its part in changing the mood and that's when the old gramophone did a great job. We had all paired off with a girl we could call a close friend, so if your close friend was down in the dumps, you would talk to her, then ask one of the other girls to put on a record. I was probably the wrong one to go to put on a 'cheer me up' record, because I could recover from bad news very quickly. Sort of down one minute and bounce back the next. I wasn't born to be miserable. When I was asked, I would make a careful selection, place it on the turntable, wind the handle and put the needle on the record. When the girls heard the tune *Home Sweet Home* the whole room would start sobbing. The song was right: 'There's no place like home'. After a while we would look around at each other and laugh at how silly we all looked. Could this be reverse psychology in action?

The nights that a few of us had a little money, we would go to one of the three little pubs in the village. *The White Hart* was our favourite. We would buy a small cider because that was the cheapest. I found out, years later, that there is nothing in the world to equal the atmosphere of an English country pub: low ceilings, small bars and walls that had soaked up the smell of beer, wine and tobacco for hundreds of years.

We sat on bench seats fitted around a small bay window, and put our drinks on a small round table. The landlord was well rounded with a pleasant reddish-brown face. He had a smile to greet every customer, and the strongest Devon accent I had ever heard. He said, 'Eve'nin' zir,' as the customers came in. The bar was only supported by a few regulars during the week. They talked about farms, farming or farm animals, unless it was the weather. If they were aware that the war was still on it wasn't mentioned. A small group were playing crib and we all laughed as they counted the score: 'Fifteen two, fifteen four, and one for his knob.'

We would sit in the pub for a couple of hours with just one drink, enjoying the atmosphere. Even though it wasn't righteous, we loved it. We talked about that crib score but didn't ask anyone what it meant, as they were all men. It might be too embarrassing to ask 'What's one for his knob?'

Lots of things that we take for granted today were unavailable or in short supply during the war. One of the hard-to-get items was make-up, and even then there wasn't a lot of choice. A group of girls like us would discuss the supply problems and the different ways that we could use the make-up we could get. At that time, society ladies and film stars used to have a beauty spot on their face to enhance their facial appearance. I was one of the lucky ones who had a mole growing naturally in the middle of my left cheek. When little Doris noticed it, she said, 'That looks smashing, why don't we all have a beauty spot?' They all thought it was a good idea and on went the thinking caps. Then little Doris came up with the idea of making them for all the girls. She took the tops of winkles and dried them. Then when they were going out, they just stuck them on their face in the position that they chose. Each time the girls made up to go out to somewhere special, they followed high fashion of 1944 and stuck on the beauty spots.

The girls were never mistaken for film stars or high society ladies when they wore them, but then winkle tops would have cost considerably less than the real thing.

CHAPTER 8

OH WHAT A SHOW

S aturday night was the big night for the land girls who liked dancing. I was one of those who loved it and always looked forward to going to the Town Hall dance and Charlie Bissett's band. These dances were always well attended by the local girls and the men who had not been called up. The main bulk of the crowd who came were service men and women who were stationed all around North Tawton. These men were attached to the Allied Forces and came from America, Canada, Australia, Norway, Poland and several other countries. Apart from us, there were land girls from other villages nearby. They weren't as easy to spot because we were allowed to wear civilian clothes: Army, Navy and Air Force personnel had to wear their uniforms.

We all loved ballroom dancing and treated it as an art that we wanted to improve upon. We created our own happy atmosphere on the dance floor and didn't need anything except the music and a partner to glide around the floor with. There was no drink allowed (or needed) inside the dance hall, and very few went up to the pub in case they missed some of the music. There was usually an MC who announced the next dance, but he wasn't ever called upon to sort out bad behaviour. We had an unwritten code that made us behave like ladies and gentlemen. It's such a pity that the young people of today can't share the comradeship and ethics that we enjoyed during the war. We had consideration for others and had no place for selfishness or jealousy.

Every now and again, we would be granted permission to use our van to go to a dance in Okehampton, always provided that there was enough petrol to take us there. This was a big occasion for us as Okehampton was one of the larger market towns in Devon. Our meeting place would be in the Square as usual, and the excitement grew as we donned our finery and walked up the hill. There would be Vi, Rose, Pauline and me and we felt good and looked good. We were all slim, attractive and very tastefully dressed.

Lace curtains would move as we passed the cottages, so we knew that the people inside were looking at us. To make sure that they weren't disappointed, we would each curtsey, but the curtains never curtsied back. We got into the van and sat on our usual seats like budgies on a perch. I suppose we are all creatures of habit.

We drove off and once clear of the village we would laugh and sing to make the journey shorter. Going to Oakhampton was like going to a big city after being in North Tawton. When we pulled up in the middle of the main street, passers-by would stop and stare and net curtains were pulled aside to see such an unusual spectacle. It must have looked really funny to see so many well-dressed young ladies climbing down a ladder slung from the back of an old baker's van. If we arrived early, we would go for a drink at one of the little pubs, as we couldn't stand in a group on the pavement, could we?

Once the dance commenced, we were on the floor straight away and didn't leave until the band played the Anthem and the music stopped. There was no such thing as going out of the hall and we only went to the toilet between dances when the music stopped. Driving home in the van we talked about who we had met, pulled each other's leg about a good-looking chap or some creep, and of course we sang. There were some very good singing voices amongst us and we put everything into the loud, fast songs, but we sounded our best with quiet songs that we harmonized with real feeling: songs like *Down in the Valley* and *Where or When*.

As we neared the village, Hilda would say, 'Be quiet now, girls, a mile to go.' We always stopped singing as we didn't want to upset the local people.

Each time we went out, Auntie would say, 'Goodbye girlies,' to Vi and me and would always add, 'Come back respectable.' We would reply,

'Yes we will, Auntie,' and of course we always did. Auntie Lil had been a complete stranger to me before I came to North Tawton, but she cared for us better than most mothers would do. She was a very proud lady and guided us as if we were her own family.

From time to time there would be a dance held at one of the service bases close by. These were always top-class events and were well organized. A big dance such as this was hosted by the Allied Forces either as one nation, such as the Americans, or several smaller nations that had a similar complement of troops. The reason that there were different hosts merely decided which funds the bills were paid from, but that didn't bother us. It was very important that we got invited because it was a superb night out.

The formal invitation would come a few days before, and it would give date, time and transport arrangements. We were usually picked up and brought home by a service truck; although, on one occasion several of us girls walked the seven miles to Winkleigh and danced all night. However, we did get a lift home. On the night of a big dance we tried every way we could to finish work early but never did. I had made a special friend of Pauline who lived next door to our little cottage. She would take hours to put her make-up on and get ready. It's a wonder we didn't miss the truck going to the dance but I always waited for her. Mind you, she looked pretty good when she was ready as she was tall and slim with blonde hair. We all looked quite glamorous in our civvies going to a dance, which was the reason we got invited. We would often swap clothes with each other because all of the girls were a similar build.

I had a lot of elegant clothes which my Nan had made me. I asked Vi to take her pick and borrow one on this occasion. She was so grateful you would think I was offering her the Crown Jewels. Her first choice was a tight-fitting dress that had been specially tailored to my slim figure. Vi was a little bigger and of course it wouldn't button up, so she settled for a dress with a fuller cut.

Our hosts for tonight were the Americans who were delighted to see us and were so polite in the way they welcomed us. There were other land girls there, whom we recognized, and a lot of local girls. Their faces were a sight to see when they saw the North Tawton glamour contingent. Nothing was said but we could see in their eyes that they were jealous of us as competition. They also knew how well we all danced.

The American dance band was really something to hear and witness. Every member was a first-class musician and many of them had played in the professional Big Bands in America. This band had based its sound on the Glen Miller Orchestra and played swing music, slow blues and the exciting jitterbug. I didn't dance to the jitterbug sound but I enjoyed watching those who did.

The band on this occasion was big and so was the sound: the musicians sat in rows on the stage that went up in several levels. On the platform at the top sat the drummer with a large array of drums and cymbals. Being played on the other levels were trumpets, saxophones, clarinets and trombones. To support the drums in the rhythm section was the piano and double bass. They could play anything, so the variation was terrific. All bands at that time had a singer: this band had male and female lead singers and three men who sang in harmony. About eighteen people in all formed the Big Band. All of these dances were good and this one was no exception. We swung to the quick step, glided to the waltz and smooched to the blues. What a night.

There was always a stir in the hall when the *Jitterbug* was announced. It was spectacular, acrobatic and very difficult to do well. Most of the crowd became spectators and only a few couples attempted this exciting dance. Pauline was wearing a scarlet dress that contrasted her blonde hair as it shone under the lights. She was partnered by an American airman named Hank, and was he good. Pauline matched every step and move that Hank made as he jived, twisted, bounced and threw her in every direction. The other dancers stood and watched, as these two were so good together that the band felt the excitement and blasted out the music, harder and louder, while all eyes were on Pauline and Hank. They finished to spontaneous applause which they richly deserved. I couldn't help thinking that the band, the dancers and the jitterbugging were so good that we could have been in Times Square. New York had been brought right here to Devon.

Getting up going to work the next morning was not easy. It had taken quite a while for the adrenaline to settle down before we went to sleep. Morning seemed to come a few minutes after we dropped off.

As the van set off to pick up Jack there was less talk than usual. Jack climbed in and told us that we were doing a fill-in job today as our other job wasn't ready. His announcement was met with silence as none of us were interested enough to ask what it was. Jack asked about the dance, but only heard a watered-down version of what it was like. Being tired, we were more inclined to describe everything with one word: 'Smashing'.

The van stopped at the barn next to the gate leading to a freshly turned field. We put our lunch tins, flasks and the other bits into the barn and went into the field. A tractor had dragged a square frame over the ground to pull up the loose roots. An empty cart to be loaded with roots stood to one side of the field. We asked Jack to put the cart a bit further along the field: it would be filled quicker if it were closer to where we picked the roots up. The tractor still hadn't arrived, so Jack tried to pull the cart. He couldn't quite manage it on his own, then he said, 'Come on, maids. If you all give it all little push we can get it in place.'

The girls slowly gathered at the back of the cart, moaning and complaining as they came. When we were all in place, Jack said, 'Right, push.' The cart rolled one foot forward and then one foot back. Just as well it *didn't* roll forward because we were only leaning on it and would have all fallen over. Then Jack said, 'Come on, maids, put your backs into it and push harder. Right, push.' I noticed Joan had grunted to give the impression that she was straining every muscle, but she wasn't touching the cart. I grabbed her hand and placed it under mine on the cart as Jack said, 'Right, once more.' This time we all made a loud straining noise, and miraculously the cart moved. We rolled it about 50 feet, ready for filling. By this time we had all woken up and Jack had his ears chewed off as we all complained. Rose asked, 'What do you think we are – pack-horses?' Little Doris said, 'Can't we do another job?' while Pauline said, 'Can't we all go home?' Then I explained that we had trouble moving it empty, so we would never move it full. Jack was assessing his position and knew that he would never win.

'All right, all right,' he said, 'I'll go up to the barn and get the tractor, while you maids start chucking in the roots.' At least our position had improved from a few minutes before.

Jack set off on foot up the road in search of the tractor, very glad to escape the moaning. As he went I thought, I bet he brings another cart for us to fill while he empties the first one.

It took us quite a while to have a smoke, look at the job and weigh up the situation. When we all decided there was no way out, we started the brain-teasing job of chucking roots into the cart. It was going to be one of those days. Everyone was moaning and cursing as they worked, then all of a sudden the mood changed as if someone had sprinkled the gang with magic dust. Well they had really. Loud cheering broke out as someone shouted out, 'Rain, rain.' It bucketed down. None of us got very wet: the rain had converted us from sluggish land girls to scampering whippets, as we dashed for the barn. The heavy showers kept up all day with the exception of one small lull. We were going to sit tight and make out that we hadn't noticed it had stopped. We heard the tractor in the lane which meant that Jack was coming back. We looked as if we were working when he arrived. And yes, I was right: he was towing another cart which he dropped off, then drove the tractor back to the farm. He hadn't gone far when the rain started again. We had no alternative: amid another burst of cheers, 'Quick, girls, back to the barn.'

On bad rainy days we had to shelter till the rain stopped. Jack always tried to get us a barn for shelter, because sitting it out in the van wasn't comfortable. We also think he arranged this so he could go somewhere else on the farm out of our way. A barn gave so much more room to move around and usually had bales of hay or straw to sit on. We would hold an impromptu concert to amuse ourselves. These concerts were organized by little Doris, probably because she was the eldest girl by a couple of years. She also had a keen organizing ability to produce a show and a lovely singing voice to take part in it as well.

We didn't need a stage, curtain, lights or a big orchestra. We held a pitchfork up to our mouths to act as a microphone and sung a bit louder.

One of my favourite numbers was *Chattanooga Choo Choo*, sung by four of us in harmony. This song was made famous by the top American female singing trio, the Andrews sisters. We weren't quite as good as them, but on these occasions were thought we were pretty close. We grouped around the pitchfork and sang with gusto. It is surprising how much talent there was amongst twelve girls: as well as singing, we had drama, poetry, sketches, monologues, comedians and dancers. One girl even claimed to be a belly-dancer. She wasn't willing to uncover her talent on cold rainy days, so we never saw what she could do. Every act got loud applause and sometimes cheers and whistles from the twelve girls present. To get volume to our ovations the groups of performers had to applaud each other to make up for the small audience. These concerts became a rainy day speciality and were very polished under the direction of little Doris. We were so pleased with our shows that we thought we could put on a concert in the North Tawton Town Hall in aid of the Red Cross. There was enough talent and items to fill a whole show on our own, so we practised our skills towards this goal. All our ideas were discussed and a programme worked out.

There were a couple of girls who were shy of the stage, so we needed a big scene to include them with all the girls, then Rose threw in an idea which was eagerly agreed upon by all. Rose was from London and sang all the Cockney songs as well as those on the hit parade. She also impersonated the barrow boys in the London markets with her lines like, 'Three for tuppence, the last two beetroots', or 'I'm not here to be laughed at, chaffed at or any other at, I'm here to sell my pills'. Then she would give long explanations of what these wonderful pills would do for you.

Rose's idea was to have a Covent Garden theme in which we all took part in the final scene. One girl didn't aspire to the limelight, but did agree to be in the crowd scene. Her part was to hold a saucer and walk across the stage selling from it. The first try didn't impress anyone because no one knew what she was selling. The part was then improved by getting her to walk across the front of the stage, holding her saucer and saying, 'Horseradish, horseradish'. She was very quietly spoken, and in the first try at a speaking part, we said, 'Speak up,' or 'We can't hear you,' to lots of laughter. She would blush and say, 'No, I'm not going to be in it.' The rest of us said, 'Well you've got to be in it, because you're one of us and we're all in it.'

Pauline and I were to do a tap dance. It was very difficult to tap dance in a barn with a cement or mud floor. Our boots would also have to be changed for tap shoes, so we couldn't practise in rain-stopped working time, although we did try. Our main achievement was to work out steps and movement. As kids we had both had tap-dancing experience, so it was a bit easier for us when we practised at the club. We never did put the big concert on at the Town Hall but Pauline and I did do a tap dance duet there in another Charity Concert. We danced to the tune of *My Ideal* which was a romantic boy and girl song. Pauline was dressed as the man and I was the lady. We had been loaned the clothes to perform in and I was wearing a beautiful, long white gown. I was used to well-fitted clothes but this dress was luxury. It had been loaned to me by the people in the big house where we had our bath each Saturday. It was tailored to be body hugging to just above the knees, then the full-length skirt flared out to the ground. As I twisted and turned to the music the flared skirt swung like a bell. With a fast twist, the fullness of the material caused it to rise to a horizontal circle. The dance went down very well with the audience and even the other land girls said they were proud of us.

CHAPTER 9

OUR OWN REGAL LADY

I was due to go home on leave at the weekend and I wanted to take a present to my Nan. If only I could get a couple of eggs, I thought. That would be a big treat for her and Granddad as eggs were rationed to one each per week. They would also be small, and light to carry. It wouldn't be easy as eggs were hard to get even in the country. That evening I had gone to the *Ring of Bells* pub with some of the girls before going on to the club.

As we sipped our drinks, Robert, the young son of a farmer, came in. We bought him a small drink just as we often did, and we all sat around talking. As we finished our drinks the girls got up to meet some of the others at our club; it was only a short walk down the road. I hesitated leaving the pub and moved around to sit next to Robert and said to him, 'Do you think you could get me any eggs to take home at the end of the week?' He looked at me and thought for a while. After what seemed like a long time he said to me, 'I'll try.' Then he quickly added, 'Whatever you do, don't mention it to the other girls.' I assured him that I wouldn't ever do that. He was only a young chap, about eighteen, who had learned to be careful in what he promised to do.

He told me to meet him in the pub tomorrow night. 'All right,' I said, and left to catch up with the other girls at the club. I felt all excited at work the next day, hoping that I would get a couple of eggs to take home. That evening I made some kind of excuse to the girls and said that I wouldn't be long. I couldn't get to the pub quick enough and found that I had arrived first. I sat there waiting for what seemed ages. Then suddenly

50

in he came looking all around him as if he was on a secret mission. Well, I suppose he was really, but he didn't look like a spy. He sat very close to me as a grin spread over his face and he nodded. 'Look what I've got,' he said in a low whisper. When I looked at what was in his hands, there were six eggs. I couldn't believe my eyes. Not two, as I had expected, but six. The surprise could not have been greater if I had been looking at gold dust. I could hardly contain myself as I said, 'Oh Robert, you are so kind, how much do I owe you?' 'Nothing, m'dear,' he replied, talking like a real old farmer, 'just give me a kiss.'

Now that was a price much higher than I had expected. He was a nice enough chap but I knew I couldn't kiss him for all the tea in China. You see, he had a rubbery sort of mouth that was always wet; just like a cow's. This called for some very quick thinking, so with a smile on my face I said, 'Oh, Robert, I can't give you a kiss because my boyfriend is miles away on a ship serving the war effort and I am saving myself for him.' He looked upset and disappointed, but gallantly said he understood how I felt. What a relief that was. He still wouldn't take the money I offered. So after all that I got the eggs for nothing.

When I left the pub with the eggs I went back to the little cottage, crept up the stairs and put the eggs into my case. The case wasn't very big so the eggs had to be well wrapped and packed to avoid breaking them. I must have made a good job of packing the eggs because they were still intact when I unpacked them at home. This was a pleasing result, so I gave my Nan two, my Mum two, and Leslie's Mum two. It was such a surprise for them all and easy to see how happy they were. Everyone remarked upon how well I looked: rosy cheeks, nice and healthy and how they thought that I had filled out a little bit. I didn't tell anyone that I would have filled out a lot more if I had continued to eat the Slingers.

Our lunches consisted of the sandwiches that the other girls had and lovely homemade cakes that accompanied the Slingers. By swapping the food around we had enough to eat without the Slingers. One of the girls called Birdie was always keen to swap because she had cheese sandwiches every day. It was good the way we all shared our lunches so that no one went hungry.

Getting back to North Tawton after going on a week's leave to London was like stepping backwards in time. I think the biggest contrast was the slow pace of the country. But one thing that wasn't slow was getting back to work.

We got off the train on Sunday night, and reported for work in the Square at 8 a.m. on Monday. Rose, Pauline, Vi and I walked up the hill to meet the van as usual. We were met with laughter and excitement by two of the girls. They had been to the van and decided to come and meet us instead of climbing in. We were greeted with, 'You'll never guess, you'll never ever guess what we've got.' No matter what we thought of they just said, 'No'. As we walked on the van came into view. Tied on top of the van, on its side, was a corrugated iron toilet. It must have been 8 foot high and 3 foot square, complete with a sloping roof and a door. It was attracting a lot of attention and loads of laughter as we all talked about who would Christen it.

Several weeks earlier, we were doing one of those back-aching jobs, picking up stones and rocks and throwing them into heaps. It was right on the edge of Dartmoor and a cold wind was cutting across the Moors. Pauline asked to go to the toilet. This may have been a genuine request to relieve her bladder or it could have been merely to get a rest and relieve her aching back. There were Italian prisoners of war working in the district, so the rule was that one girl couldn't go alone: I said that I would go with her. We walked about half a mile before selecting a spot, making sure that we took our time.

It was there that I was able to ask Pauline how she managed when she had her periods. When we were working right out in the wild, we couldn't go all day without changing. We couldn't very well take the sanitary towel home and burn it as it would be too long. It was a very important part of life and personal comfort for the land girls, but Pauline had found a solution. She found a suitable stick and pushed the soiled towel down a rabbit burrow and said, 'Here you are, bunny, here's a present for you today.' It doesn't sound a particularly nice thing to do but, if you study the alternative, what else could we do?

None of us liked the lack of toilet arrangements, so as we sat in the van at lunch one day we decided on a plan. We would speak to the supervisor next time he came. He was a big fat man, very jolly and nice and polite, when you spoke to him. Next time he arrived on the job, we all gathered around him and little Doris, speaking for all of us, said, 'Can we ask you something?' He was on the defensive immediately and said, 'You girls always want something. What is it this time?' The proposition was put to him. 'This is very important. We do think that we are entitled to have a portable toilet,' to which he replied, 'Well, you have managed all right so far.' Then we all joined in with remarks like, 'It is awkward, we are not used to this. It's all right for you, and not a bit ladylike.' 'All right, all right, I'll see what I can do.' Poor devil, he had no hope of trying to take on twelve land girls by himself. Although Jack had no idea of what we were going to say, we didn't see where he had disappeared to. He'd probably gone for a quick widdle while no one was looking.

Not many of our requests came to anything, but we were now looking at one that had. Our own portable toilet was on the top of the old baker's van. The unusual sight of the toilet and our laughter attracted the attention of the locals and many of them simply stopped and stared.

It attracted the same attention as Hilda drove out of North Tawton and into Sampford Courtenay to pick up Jack. He heard the excitement before the van stopped and we shouted, 'Look, look what we've got, Jack.' He shook his head and muttered, 'It's all wrong, shouldn't be allowed.' We knew that Jack didn't approve. He let us know that we were lucky girls and didn't deserve anything because we were always moaning.

As we doubled back to get to the job, we passed the garage at the bottom of the hill. Hilda gave a toot to Joe and we waved out the back of the van as we went by. From my seat right at the back I could see Joe staring and scratching his head. He was a good businessman but must have been thinking about the portable toilet on top. I can't put petrol in it, I can't service it, but they can smoke in it. Or was he thinking that we had all eaten something and were likely to be taken short?

Hilda drove on and pulled up at the day's job, picking up roots. We were met by a couple of farm hands putting the cart in place. Jack got them to help him unload the toilet from the top of the van and asked us,

'Now, where do you want it?' Several of us at once said, 'Down in the corner *please*,' speaking like society ladies. The three of them lifted it on its side and carried it to the corner. They rested the bottom end on the ground and swung it upright. 'How's that?' said Jack. Pushing back a smile, Rose said, 'No, further up there and pointed to where she meant. We all had a quiet chuckle as the three of them tipped it on its side, picked it up and carried it to the place indicated. Rose had been joined by Pauline, Birdie and Joan to decide on the exact spot.

One of the young farm labourers shouted, 'Make up your minds, maids,' to which Rose shouted back, 'Want to make something out of it?' Suddenly, Nobby said, 'I don't think it's fair putting it there, put it in the middle of the field, so that we have the same distance to walk.' 'Yeah, yeah,' came the chorus from all the girls. Jack and the other two men swung it over again and carried it to the centre of the field. The perfect position was checked with us before they finally pushed it upright. Jack looked quite embarrassed as he muttered, 'Use the paper,' and jammed one of those hard-paper toilet rolls onto a branch in the hedge. It wasn't going to be such a bad day after all, even if we did have a rotten job.

Although the three men were moaning to each other about us, I'm sure that they didn't realize that we had been taking the mickey out of them all the time. Even if it had taken a few weeks and plenty of moans and groans from Jack, the portable toilet now stood in the middle of the field, waiting in anticipation. It was built of 3 x 3 timber to which they had added the corrugated iron roof, walls and door. The walls stopped about 18 inches from the ground to give the appearance that it was standing on legs. As it stood in all its glory in the prime central position, it looked like a *regal lady*, so that's what we decided to call it. Our admiring gaze was interrupted when Jack said, 'Come on, you buggers, let's get to work.'

After a couple of hours, one of the young lads walked towards the Regal Lady and pulled at the door. He had a bit of a job to open it at first, as it was sticking. He managed to get it open and went inside. This was to be the first customer, and there was no charge. We gave him a few minutes and then one girl shouted, 'We know who's in there.' Then a chorus joined in. 'We know who's in there,' or, 'We can see your boots.'

Poor bloke, he was so embarrassed with our remarks and must have labelled us the unruly land girls. Jack didn't make any comment or stick up for him.

Just before the lunch break, Jack took the toilet roll from its peg on the hedge, ambled over to the Regal Lady and shut himself in. He was to be customer number two. All the girls waited a little while. It only takes a nod and wink to talk silently. When we saw his braces dangling around his feet we started to throw everything we could pick up from the ground. As these stones and pebbles crashed onto the tin, the metallic sound registered a direct hit. The swearing and the shouting let out by Jack inside was made louder by the tin giving out a sort of echo-chamber effect. In his confusion, brought about by temper, he dropped the toilet roll. It bounced off his boot and onto the field through the 18-inch gap at the bottom. He must have been holding onto the end of it and tried to pull it back, but the wind caught it and blew it out like a big white steamer.

We couldn't hear Jack's curses as we were laughing too much, but perhaps that was for the best. We did hear him when he came out of the door and shouted, 'That's it, that's the finish.' His face had to be seen to be believed: red with temper and flushed with embarrassment, his eyes sticking out like a frog, and his mouth wet with saliva. He waved his hands about and swore that he was going to have it all taken away, and added, 'You're not going to have it any more.' Obviously something had upset him.

The next morning the Regal Lady wasn't on top of the van. Possibly because it had gone for a redesign, so that the walls reached the ground. Not a word was said as to why it wasn't there, but we felt sure that we knew the reason. Then, we asked ourselves, had it been Christened? The young farm labourer must have been put right off by our remarks. Jack didn't have time before the bombardment started and none of the girls had had the courage to go into it. We never saw the Regal Lady again, so the Christening ceremony must have been carried out without our help. That's disgraceful really, after all the trouble we had gone to, to get it constructed and erected. The toilet roll that hung on the hedge was not recovered after it blew in the wind. In fact it was the first and last toilet roll ever issued to us.

Paper handkerchiefs and tissues had not been invented then: toilet paper, country style, was to cut up a piece of newspaper into 6-inch squares, make a hole in the corner big enough to thread a piece of string through to hold all the sheets together, then tie the string into a loop which allowed it to hang on a nail in the outside toilet. Of course the newspaper was never cut up until everyone had read it. You can say that for once we had it all, it had all gone now, ah well. We went behind the bush and used envelopes from our letters before the Regal Lady came so it was right back to rock bottom again for us.

CHAPTER 10

THE VOLUNTEER

The day we started on threshing we were left in no doubt as to what it would be like, being told that it would be *all work and more work.* We only had the threshing machine for a short time, so we had to work to a strict timetable to complete our quota. The threshing machine was a big, power driven monster which separated the grain from the straw and husks. Like most farm machines, it needed a team of workers to keep it working to capacity. What was meant by working to capacity was for a team of labourers to feed it as fast as it would take it. Some of us would be on top of the corn stack pitching the sheaves down to the girls below; others would feed the sheaves into the machine at a steady rate, working to the throb of the engine. This was an important job, as the supply into the machine had to be continuous and even. Two of us were at the back of the machine raking back the straw and husks from the outlet: this prevented it from choking up and kept it running smoothly. The quantity of straw and husks built up very quickly so more girls raked away the heap as we pulled it from the outlet.

We were luckier than a lot of teams because we had a full complement to keep the machine fed and cleared. Consequently, once we settled in, we kept it working to its full capacity. We had our usual morning break and it was lovely to be out of the noise and the dust for a few minutes, when the machine stopped. The whole gang had to stop at the same time, because the machine needed a team effort.

It was a beautiful day when we started work again, but by lunchtime it was really getting hot. This added to our discomfort, as we got hot and sweaty, causing the dust to stick to our skins. Some of the husks that flew in the air found its way inside our clothes and made us itch. Most of all it gave everyone an unquenchable thirst, so by lunchtime most of our flasks were empty and there was very little left to drink. Everyone was thirsty, but those who had saved a little drink wanted to keep it for later on.

As we all sat in the shade, one of the girls spoke the thoughts of us all. 'Cor, it would be lovely to have some water.' Lying flat on her back, Rose said, 'Who's going to volunteer?' Everyone kept very quiet. I thought I would rather be walking down a country road looking for water than standing in all that dust. I put my hand up slowly and said, 'I'll go.' Everyone was delighted that I had come forward in their hour of need. Some said in disbelief, 'Would you really, Marg?' and others said, 'Oh, you are kind,' in total admiration. So I told them the conditions. 'I'll tell you what, I'll need some kind of reward for going.' When asked what I meant, I said, 'Well, what about one fag from each of you?' It wasn't much, so they all agreed.

'Give me the fags first,' I told them, and started collecting one fag from each of them. The men with the machine and Jack all forked out a cigarette each. I picked up two big containers and asked Jack which way I should walk. 'Down there, m'dear, you should find a farmhouse, not very far.' I knew how far a country mile could be, but didn't mind. I was still very hot as I trotted off. I got further away as the dust and noise started up again.

Walking about a half a mile or so I came to a little farm cottage and knocked on the door. A lovely little lady opened it and said, 'Hello, dear.' I said, 'I hope you don't mind me knocking but could you give me some water, please?' then went on to explain that we were doing the threshing just up the road, and told her that the work and the heat had made us so thirsty. She said, 'Yes, come in, dear, and sit down.' As I did she said, 'Would you like a glass of milk?' to which I replied, 'Oh, yes please.' She disappeared for a short while and I thought, this is good, as I sat and waited. When she came back she was carrying a beautiful glass of milk in one hand. In the other was a plate bearing two currant buns, spread thick with jam and topped with oodles of cream. She said, 'I thought you would like these, m'dear,' as she passed me the buns, to which I replied, 'Oh, you're very kind, thank you very much.'

I couldn't help thinking to myself, how on earth did she know that I had such a passion for cream buns? 'Cream's very hard to get,' I said. 'Oh, yes it is, you mustn't tell the other girls about that,' she said, so I said, 'Oh no, I wouldn't do that,' and of course I really meant it, didn't I? I ate the lovely buns and drank the milk, being careful to wipe any suggestion of cream from my mouth. Then, picking up the containers of water, I said, 'Thank you very much,' once again. 'That's all right, my dear, come any time,' she said, 'I know you have to work very hard on the threshing machine. I'm here every day while you're threshing.' For a lady alone in a farm cottage, she seemed to have a very good understanding of the work and needs of land girls; especially mine. I picked up the heavy water containers and walked back up the road. There was a lilt in my step even with the weight of the water, as I went back to the gang. I couldn't help thinking, 'Well that was well worth it, wasn't it?'

The gang and the men couldn't thank me enough as they washed away the dust with the water I had carried. The water lasted us till late in the day. As the heat went out of the sun, on the last break, one of the girls said, 'You're a real brick, Marg. Do you think you would go for the water tomorrow?' I considered this. 'Well yes, but I would still have to have the same fag from you all.' They all said 'Yes' to the fag, and one of them added, 'But you don't mind doing it, do you?' So I reassured them by saying, 'No, not at all, I don't mind.' And do you know I really meant it.

That night at the club I kept chuckling to myself about the cream buns. If only they knew. Vi asked me what I was laughing at, I just said, 'Oh, just my thoughts.' 'What are you thinking about?' Vi said. I answered, 'I'm not telling you, they're private.' To which Vi said, 'Oh, all right then, don't.' If I had told the girls that night, I'm sure they would have pummelled me harder than that threshing machine hitting the sheaves of corn.

Next morning we were back at our positions at the threshing machine. We soon got into a steady rhythm as the hungry monster was fed to capacity. The two of us were raking the waste as it spewed from the outlet. Within minutes, the dust and flying chaff were accompanied by the noise of the engine reminding us of the warning given yesterday morning. 'It will be *work, work and more work.*' This assessment of the job was very true as we all laboured away in unison.

At the mid-morning break they all drank heartily from their flasks. They didn't mind using up the vital fluids today: everyone knew that dear old Marg would cart water later on. As we all finished lunch they all asked me if I was still going to go for the water. When I said that I would, I was given one fag from everyone, and a lot of admiring compliments. When so many people tell you how good you are you begin to believe it's true.

The lady at the farm cottage was pleased to see me. She didn't get to see many people as this was an isolated part of the country. She wanted to talk and showed me a few photographs, while I tucked into the glass of milk and buns with jam and the thick cream. We filled the water containers and I walked back to the threshing machine, and a lovely happy, smiling welcome. I was smiling too because I had a nice lot of cigarettes in my tin by this time. I couldn't help thinking, 'It's so nice of me to make so many people happy.'

The threshing continued for four and a half days. I continued to be the water carrier for all that time, as no one else would go. The girls couldn't believe that I didn't mind the daily walking to carry heavy water containers. They accepted my reasons as being that I liked to walk to keep fit, even though that was not quite true. Early in the afternoon of the fifth day I arrived back with the water just in time to see the last sheaf going through the machine. Cleaning up after the threshing was equally as dusty and dirty as doing the job, but everyone was very happy. The smiles got even bigger when the supervisor turned up. He told us that we had completed our quota in record time. I said, 'Let's all drink to that,' and passed him the water.

I have always been able to keep a secret. I wouldn't tell even under threat of terrible torture. This included secrets of others, as well as my own. Once I said that I wouldn't tell, I always kept my word. This applied to the story of the cream buns. It was a secret that I wasn't going to reveal *until I was ready.*

I remember one day Mrs Phillip who looked after our welfare, met us at the Clock Tower when we arrived home from work one afternoon, to tell us that there was to be a gathering of the land girls from the Devon districts. Some very important people would be making some speeches and awards. That was to be in a couple of days. We were given permission to use our van to get there. It would be an extra day off, so we were all for that. As she left us she said, 'Look your best, my girls. I know you won't let me down,' and of course we wouldn't. We polished, pressed and checked every bit of our uniforms the next night up at the club; took it in turns to dress and parade so that the other girls could comment.

When we left the club that night, we felt very pleased with ourselves. When Auntie Lil bade us farewell the next day, she looked very proud of her girlies. Vi and I felt good too. Even Auntie May and Pop from next door were grinning all over their faces, seeing Rose and Pauline off. Even if I say so myself, we all looked smashing. Of course we gave all the little old country ladies, peeping behind their lace curtains, a bow.

During the journey we were making sure our hats were all on a slight saucy angle, all the same. We knew we were going to get refreshments and were looking forward to something different to eat. We arrived in good time thanks to Hilda, the dear girl. It wasn't a very big hall; there must have been around a hundred or more land girls. We were shown to our seats half-way down. After settling in we looked around. What a lot of crumby land girls they looked. The meeting started.

On stage there were five people: two men and three women, one of which was our welfare lady, Mrs Phillip. As always, to young girls, it was very boring but after a while it got more interesting and humorous. Firstly they were giving certificates to the Land Army girls working on the diary farm for their great efforts. As each girl went forward to collect their certificate, we looked her up and down judging whether they were any better than us. No, they weren't. Some looked quite smart but most were scruffy. A real scruffy lot. Their hair looked like they had forgotten to brush it after harvesting months before. Their hats didn't look right either. One girl was very thin with a huge hat. We all had a silent nudge and giggle: as we've always said, 'If you can't fight, wear a big hat'. Their breeches were either too big or too small. Some of them had their socks around their ankles and they hadn't bothered to clean their shoes.

Some girls who were not wearing their greatcoats and had their green pullovers on had forgotten to put on their bras. How awful they looked. We were busy taking the mickey out of the other girls, when suddenly the speaker said, 'Now we come to the Gang Girls Division.' On and on he went about the gang girls. When he mentioned North Tawton we all sat up. He was saying how efficient they were getting the potatoes and their harvesting done well before time; their welfare officer never having to report them for misbehaving; and conducting themselves in a proper manner at all times. These girls, he said, were a credit to North Tawton. Mrs Phillip came and guided us onto the stage where we received a hearty round of applause. How pleased we were that we had done all that spit and polish. Mrs Phillip thanked us and said quietly, 'I knew you girls would come out tops.'

We were right in front when the eats turned up. Talk about make a pig of yourself in a ladylike manner. We had a lovely feast. During the break we chatted to a lot of the other girls. You could see them looking us up and down just as we had done, but they were looking at something worthwhile. We were snobs, maybe, but that's how we behaved. It was a different story when we hopped into our van to go home. Out came the fags and we had a good laugh and a swear about the crumby lot we had met that day. 'Yes,' we said, 'we land girls are doing a very important job.' After all, we were all volunteers, but we weren't recognized as the Armed Forces were. The fighting we were doing was providing the food for the hungry British people, as the Merchant Navy men were too.

CHAPTER 11

LOVERS' MEETING

There was always plenty of excitement when we were going home on leave. This time we were lucky enough to get a compartment to take all of us who were going to London. Once there we went our different ways. It was easy to see how happy we were as we laughed, chatted and all joined in singing songs. We had all gone to a lot of trouble to make sure that our uniforms were pressed, polished and smartly worn. The toughest sergeant major in the world would have to admit we were well turned-out.

As one of the songs ended, Rose said, 'You know, you were a real brick because of what you did,' and several of the other girls said, 'Yeah, you were, Marg.' 'What do you mean,' I asked, although I knew what they were talking about. Rose continued, 'I know that we handed our fags over every day, but you still trudged down the road and carried that heavy water. You didn't really moan about it, did you?' Of course I had to agree and said, 'Well, no,' trying hard to hold back a grin. Then Nobby said, 'What are you grinning at, Marg?' As my grin got bigger, little Doris said, 'What are you grinning about, is it anything to do with the threshing?' As I said 'No', they all got interested and said, 'Come on, what is it?' By this time, laughter was bursting out of me as I thought, if only you knew: I had saved this secret until I was ready. I thought – why not: we had a long journey to go, so if I spoke now, they would have a long time to be jealous. Once I had their complete attention, I told them the truth about the water, the milk and the cream buns. Although I came out with it as quickly as I could, I gave a good description of the buns, jam and thick cream. Perhaps

63

I shouldn't have told them, I thought, as they jumped on me and said uncomplimentary things about me. They only stopped when I said to them, 'You were all too bloody lazy to go anyway. So why shouldn't I have all the treats of the cream buns and the fags?' They all saw my point but I don't think I was forgiven; not for a while anyway.

We were all excited about going home and the miles slipped by as we chatted and sang on our way to London. When we entered the outskirts of the city, we all had a tidy up of our clothes, hair and make-up. The train slowed to a stop at one of the huge platforms and we opened the carriage door and scrambled out. After we passed the ticket collector, we said 'Ta, ta', 'Cheerio' or 'Have a good leave', to each other and headed off in different directions among the crowds. Then, all of a sudden, I saw this tall, handsome young man in officer's uniform and I realized it was Les. He had been away about eighteen months and my Nan had told him I was coming home so he had come to meet me. I was so pleased and he came up and gave me a little peck. I suppose we were both a bit shy after so long, and he said, 'Let's go and have a cup of tea.'

We went into the station canteen to the usual old scene. Strange how railway station canteens have the same look about them wherever they are. Les brought the tea over to the table and sat down. As he did so, I got a packet of cigarettes out of my pocket and offered him one. Then I took one and he lit them. As we sat there smoking he said, 'You didn't smoke before I went away.' I said, 'No.' Then he said, 'And you didn't wear make-up, did you?' I replied, 'No, and I didn't bloody swear either, did I?' Although he laughed at me, I think he was a bit shocked.

I had been home for almost a week and Les and I were walking along Shrewsbury Lane at night. During the war there were no lights allowed to show after dark and this included street lights. However, towards the end of the war, the Germans bombed London with *rockets* that were self-flying with no pilot. Because of this very dim street lights were permitted in some places, and Shrewsbury Lane was one of those streets. As we walked I was thinking about what the land girls had said about waiting for Les all that time and not going out with anyone else. Then I said, 'Come and stand under this lamppost,' and he asked, 'Why?' So I said, 'Are your intentions honourable?' He said, 'What do you mean?' So I replied, 'Well, the point is I'm not going to hang around waiting for you because there are plenty more fish in the sea, you know.' He gave me a hug and a kiss and said, 'Oh well, trust you to say something like that.' We didn't say anything more on the subject but I had made my point clear, and he took me home.

On Saturday my mum gave us a Welcome Home party. Any time any of the people who were in the forces came home, they had a party. It wasn't much really because there wasn't a lot of food and we didn't drink much then. It was a lovely get-together to help us forget our troubles for a while. Several of our friends were home on leave at the same time and we all met at my mum's flat at Blackheath. It was very cold and there was light snow and ice on the ground so we stepped carefully as we all walked round for a drink at the *Green Man*. We all talked and caught up with the news and after a while we went back to the flat. My friend Jean was also on leave from her Land Army posting in Wales and she was telling Tom, my stepfather, about farm work. He pulled her leg and said that she wasn't strong enough to be a farm labourer, to which Jean replied, 'I am! I could pick you up,' and Tom said, 'Go on, try: I bet you can't.' Jean took a good grip, bent her knees, then straightened her legs. It would have been a perfect lift but her shoe slipped on the icy path and they both fell in a heap. Tom was OK but Jean had twisted her ankle and had to be helped back to the flat. She didn't do any dancing that night but she still joined in the fun.

During the evening, Les made a sign to me and I went over to him. He said he had something to show me and we went into the little bedroom next door, out of earshot of the others. He hugged and kissed me and said, 'Look, this is what I've got for you.' In his hand he was holding a little square box and I thought, 'Oh, lovely.' I opened the lid and looked inside and he said, 'Oh, you don't like it, do you?' to which I replied, 'No, not very much.' So he said, 'Well, take this one now and I'll buy you what you want when I've got more money.' The thing was that while we had been going out together I had always said to him that I wanted a platinum solitaire. I was so excited when I took the little box, but so disappointed when I looked inside, for there was this ring with two little diamonds on a gold band. It was so different to what I had wanted, and he had known all the time. I was very disappointed.

Anyway, I got over the disappointment as I always did, and still do. We had a lovely time at the party, but during the following week Les had to go back to sea and I returned to North Tawton. Of course all the girls were very pleased that I had got engaged as we swapped stories of what happened when we were on leave. The poor boy in the pub who had given me the eggs thought that I was already engaged, but I didn't worry about him anyway. I could only think about the next leave when Les and I would be together again.

Back to work the next week we were all sitting in the van by the Clock Tower. We were ready to go to pick up Jack and the two Roses at the next village, when one of the girls said, 'Oh, by the way, did you know Jack's got a new set of teeth?' We didn't know and said that we didn't know anything about it. This caused quite a topic of conversation on the way to Sampford Courtenay and before we got there we decided that we wouldn't notice that there was anything different about him: no one must breathe a word about the new teeth. We all agreed, but this proved very difficult for us when Jack came out of his little cottage and said, 'Good morning, maids,' with the biggest grin that you ever saw; a grin that was completely dominated by the flash of his pearly white teeth. We all quietly said, 'Hello, Jack,' as some turned away to hide a giggle. We had been so used to seeing Jack all gummy, with a rubbery sort of mouth, that this was a big contrast. His face was now like a horse as he was *all teeth*. As he climbed in the van and sat down, we all tried to act normally and took no notice of him. All day he was so cheerful and happy to talk to us with a big grin, but we still didn't take any notice of his teeth. All day long everyone kept quiet as if nothing had happened at all.

At the end of the day we drove back to Jack's village to drop him off at his cottage. We didn't know what he was thinking but as he climbed down the steps of the van, he looked quite mournful as he said, 'Cheerio, girls.' We all said the usual 'Ta ta, Jack,' and noticed that he had no expression on his face. The grin was gone but the teeth were still showing. As he walked away we said to Hilda, 'Don't drive off just yet,' and waited until Jack had reached the gate to his house. As he did, we shouted 'Jack'. He looked back to see us all smiling in the back of the van, and we said, 'We think you look gorgeous with your teeth.' That really made his day but all he could say was, 'You cheeky buggers.'

When our gang completed the threshing in record time we expected to be given another crop to put through the machine. Fortunately, this didn't happen as we weren't finished with the original field of grain yet. The machine had separated the sheaves into three parts: the grain, the straw and the dust waste. We didn't work on the waste again but it would have been used for something. What that was we didn't see nor did we ask. The grain was bagged up in hessian sacks that were sewn up with heavy string. Wooden shovels were used to fill the bags and we soon found out they were used in a sweeping motion like a canoe paddle.

When each bag was full it was slid out of the way to be sewn. The string was threaded into a long, bent, flat-nosed needle to sew up the open top. This was done to make an ear at each side of the bag with overhand stitches in-between. The ears were to get hold of to move the full bags. Once the bags were sewn, they were loaded onto a cart by two girls, each holding an ear and the bottom corner of the bag on opposite sides. These bags were heavy and needed a joint effort to lift and swing them onto the cart. They were then taken to the flour mills for processing. It seems unbelievable that this work was done entirely by hand. There were no machines to do it for us. Hay bales were also loaded by hand and carted to sheds. They were then unloaded again by hand and stacked out of the weather in the barn where they were later used. Country life at that time was very basic and simple, but all the hard work didn't seem to do us much harm.

Our Auntie worked very hard providing a home for Vi and me. The house was always spotless, warm and cosy and the food was excellent. She washed all the clothes by hand, heating the water by a wood-burning copper. The fire was laid and lit by Auntie every Monday morning, rain or shine. By the time we got home the clothes were dried, ironed and put away. There was never any damp washing hanging about when we got home. She had not married, but looked after us like her own children, and prior to my arrival, she had two evacuee children billeted with her as well as two land girls: the children returned to London for family reasons. Auntie was upset because they had to leave; she had become so attached to them. She kept her sadness within her and put on a brave face, which all goes to show you what a great lady she was.

We land girls had to adjust to country life too, especially for our entertainment and amusement, because there wasn't any. Televisions and portable radios were yet to be invented, so we only had the weekly dance and an occasionally charity concert to look forward to. There were cinemas in larger towns, but to attend one needed transport and money so we had to find our own amusement with the talents that we had.

Killing time on bad-weather days was always a problem. If there wasn't a handy barn to do concert practice in, we had to sit and shelter in the van. This limited us to what we could do, but we did find a variety of activities other than the sing-songs: we had to, as some days we were sitting in the back of the van all day, often in very out-of-the-way places. I recall the day that I suggested that we talk about all the other girls. The rules were simple: you started with the girl on your left and then went clockwise to the next girl. The second girl had her say when the first girl had talked about every other girl in the van. The objective of this criticism was to find out how we appeared in the other's eyes. The result was amazing as there were both good and bad comments, which amounted to praise or condemnation. Some of the good comments were, 'I like your hair-style or make-up or the way that you dress.' Others included an admiration for a sense of humour, never getting upset at the way you told someone off. Bad comments were mostly things that irritated others such as,

> 'You're too miserable too long.'
> 'You keep sniffing; use your handkerchief more.'
> 'Change your hairstyle; it looks scruffy.'
> 'Stop scratching your head.'

One girl got accused of stinking the van out with 'bowel gas' through eating rotten vegetables. We all agreed with that: there's nothing like getting to the bottom of the problem is there?

The frank talking did not cause any fist fights as we all got along very well together. We learned quite a lot about our good points and failings. Laughter dominated this session, but most of all we learned how to laugh at ourselves. I would get on Pauline's nerves because every now and again I would say, 'I think that nuns should be called up.' For National Service, nuns were classified as Reserved Occupation because of their vows to their religious order. I wasn't sure if Pauline was the only Catholic amongst us: she didn't get much support in any discussion that followed. But we never talked about religion.

Another activity when we were stuck in the van all day was to hold a jumble sale. We sold off what we had with us and this was often very interesting. Most items were small, such as lipstick, some type of make-up, curlers and scarves. Clothes were on ration and many of the other items were in short supply, but sales did take place. All the girls did like to barter for a better price and some did an exchange. Pauline usually traded in the bargain basement area with what she had to sell. Some items came out at several sales because they didn't appeal to buyers: but who would want tatty bras with no elastic or a pair of crutchless knickers? Jack never sat in the van on rainy days. We don't know where he went to but he always appeared again just before we drove back. At one time I thought that he might be sheltering under the van and could hear all that was said. But he couldn't have been or he would have made a bid for the old bras and crutchless knickers.

None of us received many letters. We couldn't expect to really, because the only ones we wrote were the ones to our boyfriends. Joan was one of the few of us who used to get parcels sent to her with cigarettes and other goodies. She was rather mean with these and wouldn't share as the rest of us did. This selfishness was more noticeable on a particular day when we were all sitting in the van. There were only a couple of cigarettes between us, so when one was passed around, one puff each was better than no puff at all. Joan had a full packet from her parcel. So we asked, 'Will you lend us one, Joan? We'll pay you back at the end of the week.' True to form she said, 'Oh no! Go away, 'op it.' So with a silent nudge and a wink we all decided to teach her a lesson. On the third nod we all pounced and started stripping her, because she was so mean. What a noise she kicked up and what an effort it was to undress her in the back of the van. I looked out the back of the van as we didn't know where Jack was. We had to consider Joan's modesty, didn't we? She decided to give up before we got her in the altogether, and handed out a few cigarettes. Can't think why. But she never refused again.

Sometimes coming home from work, Hilda would put her foot down hard on the accelerator. It usually happened as we approached a long dip in the road. She would get up enough speed going downhill to carry us up the other side without slowing down. As she did this she would shout, 'Close your eyes, girls,' and we all did. I often wondered if she closed her eyes. We never did hit anything, so she must have been a good driver. You can't just be lucky all the time.

CHAPTER 12

BEDTIME STORIES IN THE 1930s

Some evenings, after a hard day at work or in winter, Vi and I would go to bed earlier than usual. It's very restful just to lie flat and have a quite chat, usually about home. We were both brought up in the depression years, but soon found that our way of life had been so different. I was from a broken home and living with my grandparents. Times weren't good for anyone, but I was luckier than most. Although my Granddad was out of work to start with, Nan earned money with her dressmaking, working long hours every day including weekends. Our life improved quite considerably when Granddad got the Caretaker's job at Shrewsbury House. It was originally a short-term position to last six weeks, but we were there for ten years until he retired. It was from this big house that I had gone to join the Land Army.

Vi came from the other side of London and a big family. All families were short of money, but the larger ones had to make their money go further to feed more mouths. The stories Vi told me of the 1930s fascinated me. It is so hard to imagine how people could laugh at themselves in such difficult circumstances. Money was very short and spent mainly on food, usually the cheapest. When something was needed, ways were found to do without it. There was never enough money to go around. With so many families with a lot of children it was not uncommon to have four children in a double bed; often two one way and two the other, with feet to the middle. There was no heating in houses except a fire in the main living-room. Bedrooms were usually freezing in the winter, so as we lay there I would say, 'Tell me some stories about when you were a kid,' and she would usually start with, 'Oh, I remember.'

The story would describe her in a big bed, doubled up with the others on a cold night. Her father came home after a drink and settled by the fire to get warm. As he got cosy she would start crying and he would come to the bottom of the stairs and shout, 'What's the matter with you?' With a little shaky voice she would say, 'I'm cold, Dad, I'm cold.' It was intended as a way of getting attention, but he would say, 'If you don't go to sleep I'll give you something to cry about.' Believing that he had settled the matter, he would go back to his chair by the fire. She gave him enough time to settle down again. Vi would shout out, 'I'm cold! I'm cold.' This would only bring repeat of the same response from Dad. 'I'll give you something to cry about,' as he stomped on up the stairs. As soon Vi heard the footsteps she would crawl across the other kids, then slide down between the bed and the wall. Dad was quite a big man and tried to bend down underneath the bed to get hold of her, but he couldn't catch her because he couldn't get his hands far enough under the bed. He would always threaten a damn good hiding if he caught her. He knew that Vi would be freezing cold by the time he went back downstairs to his chair. All she wanted was a little warmth by the fire, but was now colder than before. She just scrambled back into bed: it didn't work out that time did it?

On another occasion, two of the children were going to the shops on Saturday morning with their mother. In the main street there would be a lot of kids lining up: they were getting ready to board a charabanc for the day's Sunday-school outing. Mum would lick her handkerchief and wipe it around the kids' faces and push them into the queue. They always managed to get on the coaches and go on the trip, but never paid.

Mum met the coach at night when it came back after a day at the seaside. There weren't many treats for kids, but a surprise day by the seaside was lovely.

Buying food for the big families, with the money being so short, was a big worry. On Saturday nights Vi went to bed early to get some sleep. She was the eldest and she had to be woken up at about 11.30 p.m. to get down the road to the market before it closed. Shops and stalls didn't open on

Sundays, so they sold off all the perishable foods at a cheaper price before midnight.

Vi was given a couple of bob to buy the biggest piece of meat she could. The meat was sold in the form of an auction, but the price came down instead of going up. The butcher would tell the gathered crowd the proper price, and then asked for less. If no one said 'Yes', he would knock a bit more off the price until someone bought. There were so many people in the same boat at that time, when someone said 'Yes' and bought a piece of meat, you had lost it. But if no one shouted 'Yes' you knew that the price would be lowered.

The butcher was asked to do all kinds of deals in those days by those who had wanted more for less money. One family butcher said that a little boy was sent by his mum to buy half a sheep's head for a shilling. It was far too cheap, but he said that he would. 'Mum said will you leave the tail on,' said the boy. But half the sheep for a shilling was more than the butcher could afford.

It doesn't take long when you work with a group of girls to find out their likes, dislikes and habits. When you also share a room with one of them it takes you less time to discover these things. Just as I noticed Auntie topped up her cocoa with hot water several times a night, I also noticed that Vi was a creature of habit. This also applied to me, doing the same thing at the same time each day. I believe that one of Vi's nightly rituals was only a habit and really not necessary, so I put it to the test. Each night we would go to the toilet outside, go to bed and talk for a while before going to sleep. Every night at this time she would say, 'I'd better have a little wee.' Then get out of bed and trickle in the chamber pot that was underneath the bed. It occurred to me that if I played a trick on her it might break her of the habit. At times it must have taken a big squeeze to get such a small trickle.

We got home from work one night and I found the right moment to be alone in the bedroom after dinner. I grabbed the chamber pot and bucket from under the washstand and hid them in the wardrobe. Once I had done this I rejoined Vi and Auntie downstairs as usual for a quiet evening. At bedtime, we went to the toilet outside, climbed the stairs and got into bed.

We talked for a while and I said, 'Well I'm going to sleep now,' to which Vi replied, 'All right. Oh, I'd better have a little tiddle first.' 'Oh, yes,' I said, 'you had better do that.' Vi got out of bed to get the pot out from my side of the bed. I could feel her leaning on the bed. She felt up and down, underneath as her hands searched for the pot. When I asked her, 'What's wrong?' she said with some urgency, 'I can't find the pot.' Still keeping calm I said, 'What do you mean you can't find the pot? It's under the bed.' Vi was still swishing her hand around under the bed and said, 'But I can't find it.' Then I said, 'It doesn't matter, leave it.' Vi said, no she couldn't, then quickly said, 'I know, I'll do it in the bucket.'

'Yes,' I said, 'do it in that, Auntie won't mind.' Vi felt under the washstand for the bucket which wasn't there. So I said, 'What on earth are you fumbling about for?' The voice from the darkness said, 'I can't find the bucket, Marg.'

'Under the washstand,' I told her.

'It's not,' came the reply.

'Perhaps Auntie forgot to bring them back upstairs,' I suggested. 'Get back into bed and forget about it, I'm tired.' Vi got back into bed, thinking she was keeping me awake. The truth was I was enjoying it and having a little chuckle to myself. I waited for about a quarter of an hour and then said, 'Still awake, Vi? Don't you want to go to the lav?'

'I can't, the pot's not there.'

'Oh no,' I said. 'Well, goodnight then.'

'Goodnight,' said Vi. I gave it a little while, then asked if she was all right.

'Yes, of course I am.' We exchanged goodnights again and settled down. After a few more minutes I said, 'You could get sick you know.'

'What do you mean?' Then I told her, my Nan always said I could be ill if I didn't go to the toilet when I wanted to. But Vi insisted, 'I don't want to go.'

'That's all right then, goodnight,' I said. She said goodnight but must have been thinking about what I had said.

'Marg, you still awake?' I was and Vi continued, 'Do you think I would be sick if I didn't go?' So I told her that she could be. Then she told me that she wouldn't want to be sick, would she.

'No,' I said. After a short pause Vi asked me, 'Would you do me a favour please?' I wasn't going to agree till I knew why and told her it depended on what it was.

'Would you come downstairs with me, out the back,' to which I replied, 'I can't do that, it's too cold.' To say it was cold was putting it mildly because that night it was bitterly cold. After Vi told me I was mean I had to say, 'Yes, I know I am. There's a lot of things I'd do for you.' Enlarging on my reasons I said, 'I'm not going out in the cold, I don't want to go.'

'I've got to go now, I feel as if I must.' She got out of bed and went down the stairs and out to the back.

When she got back into bed she was freezing, too cold to go to sleep. As she lay there warming up, she asked me, 'What shall I say to Auntie in the morning about forgetting to bring up the pot and the bucket?'

'Well you can't grumble at her,' I said. 'She's very good, you can't expect her to remember everything can you?' Next morning I had to admit what a rotten trick I had played on her. Vi was a passive girl and didn't seem to take offence. She did say that it wasn't a very nice thing to do, 'I thought I was your friend.'

'Well you are,' I said, 'I won't do it again.' When I told Auntie about it she thought I had been a naughty girl. She didn't punish me and said no more.

We still got those lovely breakfasts in bed on Sundays, but had my trick done any good, did I break the habit? Well, what do you think?

CHAPTER 13

WOODCHOPPERS' BALL

We began sorting out different things to take home. I knew Les wouldn't be home on leave. When the day arrived, there was a lot of spit and polish going on, and all the girls looked very smart in their uniforms.

A few of us had new breeches tailor-made from a kind of twill that the officers in the Army had. They were a fawn colour and looked good.

We weren't at all surprised to see the train pull up, apparently full. We managed to squeeze in and started walking through the corridors trying to find a vacant seat. Some were lucky; those who had got on the train first. In the end, Rose and I seemed to be the only two of us girls still looking. We had passed this carriage before with the blinds pulled half-way down, with the notice 'Reserved' on the windows. We sat in the corridors on our cases, and looking around noticed that inside the carriage were a couple of vacant seats. Well, we thought, that isn't right is it? We're all in the war together aren't we? As we sat peering through the glass, we tried to look tired and started to yawn. We wanted to be noticed didn't we, and of course we were.

Well here we are, a couple of nice-looking land girls wanting a couple of empty seats to sit in for the four-hour journey home and there they were on the other side of the glass: 'reserved', the notice said. After a while, we knocked on the door and a Petty Officer partly opened it.

'S'cuse us,' we said, 'are those seats reserved for anyone in particular?'

'Sorry,' he said, 'this carriage has been reserved by the Admiralty.' Then a voice from inside said, 'Don't be mean, let the poor girls have these spare seats.'

We were delighted at the offer, and the officer slid our cases in and put them on the top of the rack. When we looked around, there were six Navy men in all and we were so grateful, we offered them one of our precious cigarettes. They wouldn't hear of it and handed us a tin of their Duty-Free, which we eagerly accepted, then lit up and sat back very pleased with ourselves.

It wasn't until we settled down that we realized that two ordinary sailors were handcuffed to an officer each side of them. Rose and I nudged each other and Rose said, 'What have you got those things on for, have you done a murder or something?' Then I said, 'You must have been naughty boys then, eh?' This is the reason why the carriage was reserved by the Admiralty. But we wanted to know why they were handcuffed, and said, 'Well, what have you been up to then?' Then they explained that they were being returned to the barracks for overstaying their leave. Then I said, 'Is that all, why don't you let them go?' and Rose said, 'Yeah, take them bloody bracelets off.' Then I said, 'Yeah, we won't hurt them.' We all had a good laugh, and settled back again on our journey.

We asked them what they did in the Navy and we told them how hard our life was in the Land Army. They said they hadn't realized the type of work we girls were expected to do and how was it we still kept our sense of humour. Rose told them about Billy, her brother, being the best Marine in the Navy and I told them that Les, my boyfriend, was on a merchant ship bringing all the food home.

We avoided the serious talk about the war and how it was going, and spoke about going on leave, our little club room in North Tawton and the dances at the Town Hall and at the American bases where we met Yanks, Norwegians, Poles, Australians and many other allied forces. We were a bit tactless really when we said we didn't go for British Servicemen because they had less money, but after it was said, we thought it was just as well they were handcuffed.

Nevertheless, we all laughed and passed it off. We talked of all the wartime songs and tunes that were in the hit parade of that time, then we each said what our favourites were. Each of us had some sentimental attachment to one of the tunes, as it reminded us of someone or something.

Then one of sailors said he liked the *Woodchoppers' Ball*, played by a big band with a clarinet solo. This was a band number with no words to sing to. Then he said, 'Do you know how it goes?' No we didn't, but wasn't it la la la? No, that's not right. We all put on our thinking caps, using a few notes but couldn't get it right. None of us could get it right after many attempts.

We talked of other things and found out two of the officers were married with children and they showed us little black and white photos which we called snap shots. One came from Manchester and the other one from a little place in Wales. We did think they would be stationed at Chatham in Kent but they weren't allowed to say, so we didn't ask.

All mail to the service men was addressed to care of GPO London and it was redirected by service personnel. Of course we said, 'We hope you are being true to your wives,' and they came back, 'Hope you are being true to your boyfriends with all those Yanks and dozens or more that there are down in Devon.' The score was 1:1 (a draw).

As we pulled into a station on the way, the porter shouted out the name of the station in what seemed to be a foreign language which we couldn't understand, so it couldn't be London. All the station names had been taken down just as road signposts had. If the Germans had landed they would have had to ask the way to go. As soon as the train had stopped, one of the officers headed for the door. I said, 'Where are you going?' then quickly thought I shouldn't have asked that. He could be going to the toilet. Fortunately Rose asked if he was getting off here. He just said he was going for refreshments. I said, 'Let them go for their refreshments,' pointing towards the prisoners, 'we'll go with them to make sure they don't run away.' Rose said, 'Yeah, get them handcuffs off.' The officer said very politely that they wouldn't be doing that, but we could go with him if we liked. The offer was tempting because there might be a NAAFY canteen on the station, and their food was better. But then we thought we might lose our seats if we got up. So after a short pause we said, 'If we can't take them, we won't go.' Everybody laughed and the door to the carriage was slid open by the officer. Then Rose said, 'Don't get the top sandwich with all the dry ends curled up.'

The door closed and off he went. Rose looked at the oldest officer in the carriage and said, 'Are you in charge?' and he said he was. 'Oh, so you're the Captain then,' and he shook his head. 'Yes you are then, go on, show us your Captain's hat.' One of the prisoners said, 'Sh, tra la la la, la.' 'No, that's not it,' and we all started to thinking about the *Woodchoppers' Ball* again. We all knew it but couldn't get it out. The officer kicked on the door outside and we opened it a few inches and looked out just as the Navy man had done to us. There stood the officer with a box and cups in one hand and a flask in the other. The refreshments for the prisoners and escort had arrived. Inside the box there seemed enough food to last six men a week, which was passed to the chap in charge, who said, 'Ladies first.' What a stroke of luck, they had bought enough for us, thanks to the Admiralty. I had first pick and took a lovely fresh cheese roll and my favourite, Eccles cake. I also noticed there were no Slingers in the box. It went quiet as everyone rested back in the seats with a roll in one hand and a cake in the other and started eating.

After a while the officer poured out eight teas from the big flask and passed them around. 'Ladies first, of course.' Just then two of our land girls looked in the window below the blinds. Rose and I just put our noses in the air and turned our heads as we pulled down the blinds a little more. We decided to continue our war effort without them, even if we were on a train. After all, we were sharing our goodies with the Admiralty, so there is no way we would share the luxury with them. Even with eight mouthfuls of food someone would try to la la la. But from behind a mouthful of Eccles cake I had to say, 'No, that's not right.' The food box was passed around again; ladies first, of course. But although there was plenty left, Rose and I couldn't eat any more. I suppose it was because we were sitting down and not using up our energy with farm work. I gave a polite, 'No, thank you very much,' and said the prisoners could have my share. I don't know how long they had been on the run, but they ate a week's supply of food in less than an hour.

By this time Rose and I had the need for the call of nature, and we had previously noticed that the ladies' toilet was a short way down the corridor. Although we thought our seats were safe, we did ask the officer in charge to look after them for us. He assured us that if the Admiral himself came along he couldn't have our seats. 'That's all right then. Come on, Rose,' I said and out we went together.

Train toilets are small, so it was one inside and one outside. I went first and then Rose. As she came back into the corridor a couple of our land girls came along. We both pounced on them and said 'How does the *Woodchoppers' Ball* go?' La la la la la, then lee lee lee lee la. 'No, no good,' I said, 'ask the other girls if they know.' Then it was their turn to ask, 'Can we come in your compartment? There's plenty of room in there.' I said, 'No, sorry.' 'Why not?' was the next question. I had to think now, and it had to be good. 'Well,' I said, 'we're special guests of the Admiralty.' As Rose and I returned to our comfortable seat amongst the prisoners we realized that our compartment was First Class only. When we saw that and the door was slid open to let us ladies in, we really believed the Lord of the Admiralty had looked after us. Well, some Lord was looking after us, wasn't he? I bet he knows how the *Woodchoppers' Ball* goes. Still none of us could think of it.

As the miles slipped behind us, we found that the Navy boys were excellent company and we had so many laughs about a lot of things: who wouldn't chuckle inwardly at the treatment we had been given. Good seats, First Class of course, plenty of refreshments and an endless supply of duty-free cigarettes and we hadn't paid a thing. We thought that the Admiralty must be a very nice man.

From time to time a land girl came from our gang and knocked on our compartment door to sing, hum or whistle that elusive tune, but none of them got it right. Some didn't even get it remotely like it, but we suspect that they had only come to spy on Rose and me.

Just before we pulled into Paddington Station in London, the officer in charge asked us to stand outside as we must not be seen with the prisoners. They took our cases down from the rack and placed them in the corridor by the door. I had one last try to see if they would let the prisoners go. Rose tried a bit of sob stuff as well, but it was no good. They were probably for the high jump. All the Navy fellows thanked us for making a pleasant experience of what would otherwise have been a dreary journey.

They told us they had enjoyed our company so much. Rose and I felt real good about this and gave each of them a little kiss. Even the prisoners. Neither of them was married so I suppose that kiss made them feel like doing a bunk again. The officer in charge seemed a bit embarrassed, but I bet he loved it.

As we went out the door one of them went La la la la la, no wrong again. We stood in the corridor in the last couple of moments of the journey: more of our girls tried to hum that damned tune, but no good. I do believe that the whole train was trying to remember the *Woodchoppers' Ball*. When I hear it even now I think of those sailors and that journey.

We never got to meet our host for the ride, the Admiralty.

CHAPTER 14

SPUDS AND FAIRIES

Most of the work we took in our stride. You didn't have time to get downhearted when you were with a gang of twelve land girls; there was always at least one of us able to look on the bright side. Then Jack announced that we would be picking up potatoes the next day. There were eleven cries of, 'Oh no', plus my happy voice that said, 'That will be a nice change.'

Most of the girls had been there longer than me, so I was simply told, 'Wait until you try it,' to which I replied, 'What are you moaning at, it's something different.' Nobby said, 'It's different all right, you'll soon find that out.'

I got up bright and early next day and thought of it as just another day as we hopped into the van and drove off. Once we got into the field, we could see rows and rows of potatoes that seemed to stretch forever. We were allocated rows to work in. All we had to do was to pick up the potatoes and tip the full bucket into sacks. These were placed at intervals near the rows. The tractor was old and it wasn't well equipped either. Its job was to dig up a row of potatoes with a disk and a shield which would push them into rows; but when the tractor set off, there was no shield and the potatoes rolled everywhere. Instead of them being in heaped rows and easy to pick up, they were scattered all over the place. This meant we had to walk around picking them up.

Working like this we had to bend over and straighten up, but did that worry us? Of course it did. We all complained furiously. No one took any notice of us but we did air our point of view. At that time I wasn't really worried because I didn't know any different. The girls who had picked up potatoes before realized how much harder the job was for us without the shield.

The moans and protest continued until we stopped for lunch. It was at this work break that ideas were discussed and clever schemes hatched. Today's scheme was very secret, shared by only two, and I wasn't one of them, so when Vi and I were asked to get a bit a sugar without Auntie knowing, we hadn't any idea of the plan that was hatching. The work carried on all day. Potatoes were scattered all over the place and the moaning didn't stop either. It was a quiet sort of evening at the club that night and no one was late going to bed. It wasn't till next morning I knew why the other girls had moaned so much the day before. My back muscles had tightened and I couldn't move. When Auntie brought us up a cup of tea, Vi said, 'Marg can't move, Auntie, what shall we do with her?' Auntie looked at me and said, 'You'll be all right once you get going, dear.' That left me with no alternative. I had to crawl out of bed. This proved to be terribly painful as I forced myself to get up, wash and dress ready for work. The muscles of my back felt so tight, as if they had been tied in knots: I could only move by forcing myself through the pain and agony.

We had managed to sneak a little bit of sugar and set off to the van. When we were all sitting inside, each pair of girls handed over the sugar. We still didn't know what for. Nothing was said driving to the potato field and no questions were asked about the sugar. Those in the know had big grins which seemed to spread excitement among all of us. Courtney, the farm labourer, was already at the field waiting to drive the tractor. He was with us most days and acted as Jack's right-hand man. We worked until morning break. We all sat in our usual group away from the men. They often wandered off or were preoccupied with something else; they didn't ever worry about us until it was time to start work again. As one of the girls headed off towards the tractor, we were all told the plan. 'We're going to stop the tractor from working,' we were told in a whispered voice. This was greeted by quiet laughter as the excitement grew. Then it was announced that the sugar was in, so that only we girls could hear. We rubbed our hands in glee and puffed away on the cigarettes. Then Jack said, 'Right ho, let's get started.' There was hardly a movement as Courtney mounted the tractor, as we all thought it wouldn't start. But to our horror the engine roared into life and smoke billowed from the smelly exhaust. Our faces dropped, as someone asked, 'What's gone wrong?' Then we discovered that the sugar that should have gone into the fuel tank to gum up the engine, was put into the radiator cap. It had dropped harmlessly into the cooling water. As that tractor sped up and down the rows, potatoes seemed to be thrown even further away than ever. It kept going all day, never missing a beat. Now we know what a mechanic means when he says an engine sounds sweet.

The sweet sound of the tractor had a reverse effect on us girls; we were sour and got worse by the minute, as we endlessly picked up potatoes. Our well-planned scheme to give us some rest had gone wrong. At lunch we thought again. On this sort of job we were expected to go to the toilet as a group. This is because it was an isolated area: there were Italian prisoners of war in the area, and we all worked as a team. We usually went for a wee at the beginning of break, so we decided to change our habits. Now if we all went at the end of a break and took our time, we wouldn't be back when the clock said to start work. This was to be our extra rest.

A couple of minutes before starting time Pauline said, 'Going to the toilet, Jack.' We wouldn't care if he heard or not. We walked away from the job for a far distance, taking our time to find that special spot. We were guided by Pauline, because she had been doing this all the time and was an expert. We stopped in a clearing sheltered by trees and all agreed that this was good enough. Then, getting into formation, we all dropped breeches and squatted. We had formed a fairy circle. All facing inwards. We talked about anything, except what we were doing, but most of all we got out of a bit of work, didn't we?

In the time that the North Tawton land girls worked as a gang, the fairy circle was formed many times in many different places. A keen country observer can point these fairy circles out to you even today. Of course you won't find any fairies, but they tell me that the mushrooms still grow in rings.

My backache didn't go despite what Auntie had said, but I kept working. I expected it to go as quickly as it came, but a lot of the time I felt numbed by the pain. I worked on automatically without really noticing the potatoes that I was putting into the bucket. Then I got hold of one that seemed to stick to the ground. I pulled a bit harder and as my fingers tightened around it, I realized that it was soft and furry. It was then that I moved quicker than I had for a few days and shouted to the others. 'Ah, what is it?' Jack said, 'It's a mole's tail.' We all immediately thought of Brenda and the mouse: none of us fancied a mole up our trouser leg. It gave me the shivers, but we all laughed later on.

The weather is an important element of the day for a girl getting married. It was this element that made us all remember the wedding of Brenda, one of our land girls, to Colin, a farmer's son. Our prayers had only been answered up to a point. We didn't get rain; we didn't get sunshine. What we did get was snow. We had a medium fall overnight putting a blanket of white over everything. Fortunately there were no ice patches yet so that the roads were still in use. However, it was very cold, but not bad enough to upset the North Tawton land girls.

Brenda looked lovely as a bride and a snowy background seemed to highlight the colour on her cheeks. Never let it be said that she was blushing. Little Doris as Maid of Honour and Birdie as bridesmaid both looked beautiful in their taffeta dresses as they arrived for the ceremony.

The snow had stopped falling just before the service to allow the bride to look her best as she came down the aisle. Although a wedding is a happy occasion, there were still a few tears from the ladies as they were moved by the service. When the happy couple left the church, all the land girls formed a Guard of Honour with an archway of pitchforks. As the bride and groom entered the arch, snow started falling like a silent hail of confetti. What a beautiful picture it was and a wedding to remember. Why? Well hidden from sight under those lovely taffeta dresses, little Doris and Birdie were wearing Land Army wellies.

Farm work is different from most jobs. Just as you think, well that's finished, it isn't. When we brought in the stooks and made the stack, we didn't think that we'd have to put it all through the threshing machine. So when we picked up and bagged all those acres of potatoes, we thought we'd seen the last of them, but once again, how wrong we were. So when Jack said, 'Taters tomorra', our hearts sank into our boots and we all prayed for rain.

It was a dry, fine morning to start the new day. So the van drove us girls to where the potatoes had been temporarily stored. 'That's the Riddler,' said Jack. We turned to look without any sign of interest. We took another look, in silence, at an ordinary looking object called a Riddling machine. It was a long, shallow, wooden trough, about two foot wide. It was on a stand, and lying almost flat. There were rods and chains on funny looking wheels that connected to a drive belt underneath. Our inspection couldn't have lasted two seconds. Although none of the girls were impressed by what we saw, we all agreed it was all right if it saved us a bit of work; but we soon found out it saved us nothing.

The team was set up around the machine: two were loaders on one end; two were grading on the high side; three were bagging on the low side; three were sewing behind the baggers; and two were loading onto the lorry. We all waited to see what this motorized board would do. There were cheers and laughter as Courtney started the motor and then pulled the lever to engage the drive belt. The wooden trough that was the working bench started to move. When it was shaking backwards and forwards with a sort of roll from side to side, Jack said, 'Right, tip the bag on.' We couldn't believe it. Rose said, 'Is that all it does?' No one answered Rose's question as it got lost amid eleven other rude remarks.

The loaders tipped the first bag onto the trough and the potatoes wriggled and rolled along it. As the load flattened out, the two graders picked out the damaged and poorly shaped potatoes. This included those with skins that were green, through growing partly on top of the soil. The green was said to be poisonous, but I never tried to eat them, and lived.

Spuds were taken to the low side and dropped through holes of different sizes to grade them. The very big ones rolled off the chute at the end. At each hole, and at the end, the baggers caught the spuds in a sack and slid it to the sewers when it was full. Bags were sewn with ears, the same as corn bags; but the overhand stitches could be a lot bigger. Finally, the full bags of graded potatoes were tossed up onto the tray of the lorry and Courtney loaded them into position.

We all compared notes at the first break and decided on two things. The first was that the Riddling machine could only be designed by a German, because only the enemy could inflict so much torture on our aching backs. This was damned hard work. Our second resolution was the long-term vow of twelve overworked land girls to a future generation. We each swore that if we ever had children those kids would have to eat every bloody scrap of potato put on their plates.

We had just finished a hard day at the Riddling machine and were all seated in the back of the van. Our tiredness made us impatient as we waited for Jack to climb in and Hilda to drive home down the road. Then Jack saw another van that he had been waiting for, coming up the road. As it came closer, Hilda said, 'It's the Ities.' This was a gang of Italian prisoners of war, who also did farm work labouring like us. The driver pulled past us and parked right behind our van, about twenty feet away. The driver was a local chap and there was an English foreman just as we had. We didn't see any guards as there was nowhere to go if one did escape. The two vans were back-to-back so that we were looking at them and they were looking at us. We were in a perfect position to hold a meaningful conversation with them.

One of the girls was first to break the ice, she walked to the back of the van and leaned out. As she did so, she raised two fingers in a Victory sign and blew a loud raspberry with her tongue stuck out of her mouth. Then she said, 'You're only prisoners because you couldn't run fast enough,' accompanied by another two-fingered raspberry salute. We all forgot that we were tired and all joined in with abuse and rude orchestrated signs. They were called lazy layabouts, cowards and creeps and told that they were shifty murderers born out of wedlock. Rose told them that her Marine brother could beat hell out of a lot of them on his own, even with one hand tied behind his back.

The Italians were also tired: weren't they always tired? They also sprung into action after our first outburst. With fists clenched and waving they shouted a lot of spaghetti talk we couldn't understand. Then one girl shouted, 'Speaka da English, you dopey buggers,' as we all laughed and jeered. Then they fired a big salvo of 'Churchill no good', and gave the thumbs-down sign. Quick as a flash, the land girls retorted 'Mussolini stinks', which was joined by 24 upraised fingers and 12 loud raspberries. One Italian shook a fist and rattled off a high speed, high pitched warning in his own language. We couldn't understand him, but Rose replied, 'Yeah, you and whose army? Get lost you little squirt.'

Jack climbed in and both vans drove off. We wanted the last word so the girls were saying, 'Go on, sod off, go on, run away again,' amid cheers, jeers, two-finger salutes and raspberries. We didn't think they could hear above the macaroni talk in their van, but we felt that England had defeated them again.

The two vans sped away in opposite directions and our onslaught on the Italians didn't stop until they were out of sight. We all shook hands and patted one another on the back as we all settled down. There were wide smiling faces as we told each other how well we had done. By the time we pulled into North Tawton we had all regained our usual ladylike composure. You know I have always found Italian people to be placid and peace-loving. Wonder what upset this lot.

CHAPTER 15

CHRISTMAS PARTY FOR THE TROOPS

As we crossed off November on the calendar and went to December, we started to think of Christmas. It would be nice to go home on leave and to see our families again, to sit by the fire near the Christmas tree under the paper decorations. Then one girl thought it would be nice to invite some of the service men from the American base to a Christmas party. We had enjoyed their hospitality at those dances, so this would be a way of saying 'Thank you' to them. The plan was to have a social type of evening with a Christmas tree and decorations. The records would provide the music and we could have cakes and sandwiches, tea and coffee.

Each girl would buy a small present to hand out. Our club wasn't big enough, especially if we wanted to have a bit of a knees-up, so we got permission to use a bigger room in a business called the Pantry. This was a tea room and pastry shop and we had use of the room for the evening, but it had to be cleaned up for the business the next day. Our girls were to make the sandwiches and our Aunties made the lovely cakes. To buy tea and sugar we needed ration coupons, so we made application and got them. An invitation was sent to the American airmen and they were delighted with the idea. With most arrangements made, all we had to do was find a small present to give to our guests. This was not as easy as one would think. First of all, none of us had much money to spend, even on pay day. Secondly, we were very limited in our choice, because everything was in either short supply or unavailable, due to the war. Most novelty items were imported and our ships were too busy taking war materials to the troops. On their return, each ship was loaded with food and vital supplies because of the enemy blockade of Britain. It took hours to hunt around for something different. After a while I decided to buy a colourful ladies' garter. We weren't to tell the others what we had bought, so I hid it in my case until the party.

On the day of the party, the Pantry became a hive of industry as we did the preparations for the evening. Decoration of the room came first as we had to make our own paper chains. We used the coloured strips of paper about twelve inches long and one inch wide and stuck them in a circle. The next one was threaded through the first and stuck and so on until we had a chain. These took a long time to make as we had chains from the centre light to the corners, and from the light to the centre of the walls. We also put loops of paper chains to join where each long chain touched the walls. Just below the loops, the names of all the girls were written in cotton-wool to look like snow. We had dug up a small Christmas tree from a coppice on a nearby farm and decorated it with tinsel. The farmer was out at the time, but I'll ask him if its all right to have the tree, next time I go by.

Tables and chairs were set out while a couple of girls carried the gramophone and records from the club. They also brought with them our club visitor's book so that our visitors could sign. The visitor's book such as this can bring back a lot of lovely memories of people. Some of the remarks that were put into it were very touching. To read so many names, you can't help wishing that they all got back safely. Teapot, teacup, saucers and plates were laid out ready and we covered them with a spare tablecloth to keep the dust off. The teaspoons were arranged in a circle on one of the tables for a special reason. You see, we were all tea drinkers, but a lot of Americans drank coffee, so we put a bottle of Camp coffee syrup in the centre of the spoons. The sugar bowl was outside the circle of spoons. Our last job was to make the sandwiches and put them on plates. They wouldn't let me arrange the cakes on the plates, because they said that, after the buns, jam and cream episode, I was a pig. What a cheek! It was all ready, so we just dashed home, had a good wash and got dressed in our best party frocks.

Getting the room ready for the party had been a lot of work, but we didn't notice it because we were so excited. It doesn't need a big injection of money to enjoy life. We hadn't spent much on our party, but we all had a great time. Good job we got the bigger room, because once the gramophone started, everyone wanted to dance. Some of the servicemen had brought a few drinks, so we all had a toast to Christmas. What a lot of fun we all had doing the *Lambeth Walk*, the girls from London giving instructions to American airmen was a sight that you just had to see, and what a laugh we all had at them as they all tried to sing and dance. Their impersonation of a Cockney was a riot. They would do the swagger all right, thumbs behind their lapels, but they didn't master the words 'Doin' the Lambeth Walk, Oi.' But they were really good sports; never tried it before and wanted to do it all again.

All of the gifts bought by the girls had been wrapped in coloured paper, as fancy Christmas paper wasn't available till after the war. No one had a special partner so all the gifts were unlabled, then put into a tub and mixed up. Who had bought each gift had been kept secret from one another so we were all surprised when they were opened. It was left to little Doris to make the announcement to thank our guests for their hospitality at their wonderful dances. She also paid special tribute to the musicians in those marvellous Big Bands that we enjoyed so much. The tub was then passed to each of our guests to take a lucky dip for their present. They all waited until each of them had one and then all opened their present at the same time. As it happened, the airman I was sitting next to received my garter. He was as pleased as punch and laughed like mad as he slapped his leg and said, 'What a great gift.' He put the garter on his leg and paraded in front of all his mates. We all kept the gifts' donors secret, and of course I didn't let on that I had bought the garter. I often wondered how he explained the garter to his girlfriend when he got home, because it hadn't been issued by the American Airforce.

It was a cold winter's day as we sat in the van heading out to do one of our least favourite jobs, hedging and ditching. Christmas had been and gone, and the New Year wasn't progressing very well for us so far. New Year's resolutions had been broken by all of us weeks ago as Joe at the garage increased his sales of cigarettes that we bought. There was less space in the van as it was cluttered up with wet weather clothing. Oil-skin coats, sou'westers and wellies. It was wet but it wasn't called rain. 'It's Scotch Mist,' Jack said, as we all moaned at him. Jack really suffered when we didn't like something. Yes it was dull and misty, and very fine rain blew in the wind. We couldn't see what was Scotch about it: didn't taste of Whisky. Maybe it was called Scotch because him up there was too mean to let it pour down so we didn't have to work.

The van stopped and we all got out. We buttoned up our oilskins tight around our neck and pulled on our sou'wester hats and tied them under our chins. You don't get a second chance if the fine rain gets in: if you get wet to the skin, you're wet all day and half dead tomorrow. Realizing he was in for a hard time, Jack lit a fire so that we could burn the wood we cut down. He was a cunning old devil, and he didn't think we knew the real reason for the fire. First, we knew that he would poke it and play with it just to keep warm himself. We also knew that we had to keep chopping to build the fire up.

If you had been passing when we all had our wet-weather gear on, you couldn't tell who was who. A stranger would think we were going to launch the lifeboat and sing *Those in Peril on the Sea*. They couldn't tell if we were hymns or hers.

It got colder as the day progressed and the fine rain turned to light snow. On these cold days, the cold gets to the end bits first; feet, hands, ears and nose. Of these, it's the nose that needs the most attention as it runs. It doesn't take long to get a handkerchief soaking wet, and if you continue to use it, the nose gets very sore. There is always a limit as to how much snot you can wipe on the back of your hand. With all these waterproof clothes on there is nowhere else to wipe. So, as the mucus runs slowly from your nose towards your mouth, you do what the navvies do and blow it away. To be a good snot blower, we found that the most effective way was to throw your head sharply to one side and to blow air hard through the corner of the mouth. We all got pretty good at it and competed against each other for greatest distance.

Late in the afternoon it got bitterly cold and the fire became all smoke and no heat. For the first time Jack felt the cold, but it wasn't until a couple of the girls blew the snot at the van and it hit like a stone that Jack took notice. 'The snot turned to ice as it ran down our faces,' they told Jack. Well he'd heard it hit the van so it must be true. 'Righto, maids, we'd better get back before the roads get icy,' he said. We never told him that as the girls nodded their heads and blew the snot at the van, they also chucked two little stones at it to make the noise, but thank goodness he believed it.

People living in the city don't have the same feelings for the four seasons as the country folk. City dwellers are concerned about the weather which controls what they do and what they wear. They use their five senses to see a bus, hear it coming, smell the engine and taste the exhaust fumes, their touch is used to feel the step with their foot and their hands to grab the rail to get on the bus. This is different in the country, not because there aren't any buses, but because the country people use their five senses to read nature. This is most noticeable in the spring, although if you ask anyone when the spring starts, they can't tell you. From what I could find out, it is either early or late, but it's never on time.

In 1945 the spring was early. When I asked Jack how he knew that, he said, 'Lambing started in late February.' He then pointed out the spring shoots, the blossoms, the birds and the wildlife which was mating. These people not only use their eyes, they also listen for sounds, such as bird calls, fox barks or distant thunder. They use their noses to smell the rain, the blossom or animal traces, while their tastebuds sample berries, grain, grasses and pollen. Their touch sense is in their fingers, hands, faces, knees and feet. My tastebuds respond to cream buns, but not to a fresh, raw pea from a pod. Les, my boyfriend, said my nose was too small to do a lot of smelling. When he was on leave he kissed it and called it a button. Last leave he kissed my button nose so many times I felt like a Pearly Queen. I tried so hard to train my senses to the country ways, but only made very small progress. When I said that I heard the cuckoo in April, I was told that it had migrated from the hot climate. They lay their eggs in the nest of another breed of bird, who does the work of hatching for them, then fly abroad in late August. The birds in the invaded nest don't notice the strange eggs, but I bet when the chicks hatch out and one is different to all the others, the cock bird says to the hen, 'Ello, ello, what's all this then?'

When I asked a local to point out some of the birds to me, I became more confused. 'Now if you see a crow on its own, it's a rook, and if there's two rooks together, they're crows.' It must be that country logic. When the swallows were swooping close to the ground, I asked why. They followed the insects down, and that's a sign of rain, I was told, but some of those swallow are swifts. Oh no, another rooks and crows explanation, but it wasn't; swifts are a bit bigger than swallows and they are different from house martins. I thought, 'Oh, mate, what next?' House martins build their nests under the eaves: they collect little bits of clay in their beaks and mix it with saliva and stick it on the wall. They keep sticking these bits on until they make a hollow nest then they make a small hole to get in and out, then they mate. Fascinating birds to watch; make a lot of mess; poop all over the place, you know.

There's so much these people know about the country, I thought I would never learn. Each time I take a deep breath on a farm to get that lovely country smell I come up with the same description, 'Ah, wood smoke and cow shit,' but I'll still keep trying.

Nan and Granddad had been evacuated to Coombe Martin in Devon following their retirement from Shrewsbury House. With them was my sister and her baby son. At that time it was government policy to evacuate young mothers, children and the elderly from London to ease the strain on the war-torn city. Having family so close to where I was in North Tawton gave me the opportunity to visit them at weekends. I didn't feel so far away once they arrived here. Granddad was very unsettled there for a while, worrying about Shrewsbury House. He always looked upon it as his house, his mansion and his castle, because he and Nan had been so dedicated to it. It was a big change for him. He found it hard to change the live-in routine of the keeper of the keys. It was equally as difficult for Nan, knowing she had left a lovely home for good, never to return. My sister and the baby had spent some time evacuated to other places. They were not so attached to the big house, having previously made the break.

Arrangements had been made for me to visit them one weekend, and I looked forward to it all the week at work. I always have great pleasure in having something to look forward to, often anticipating what I would do or say, and what it would be like.

On the Thursday before the weekend we had finished work and had our dinner. Auntie had left Vi and me in order to attend the weekly meeting of the Women's Institute. This was a nationwide association of country women from all walks of life. They met to share experiences and help others. Once we had the home to ourselves, I asked Vi if she would look at the top of my head, because I had a terrible itch. It needed someone else to look because I couldn't see it in the mirror. As I sat down, Vi asked me where it itched. Now that my attention was focused on it, I felt as if it itched all over. I said, 'Just around here,' pointing to an area around the crown. Vi eased my hair apart where I had indicated. 'I can see a red spot, I'll get a comb.' Using the comb to hold my hair aside, Vi could see a strip of skin on my head. Then she said, 'You've got crawlies, I'll catch one.' 'Ooh! what do you mean?' to which Vi replied, 'I think they are fleas.' She caught one and put it on my writing pad. It jumped, so there was no doubt about it: I had got fleas in the head. It's difficult to describe how dirty I felt after being told that. We were told as kids that we could avoid getting fleas by keeping ourselves and our clothes clean. I had done this and still managed to get them. I felt disgraced in the same way as when the Health Nurse came to school and found nits on other kids. Everyone called her Nitty Nora when she wasn't listening. She had steel combs in a dish that was filled with carbolic and hot water. Carbolic was a disinfectant that the combs were dipped into after each child had had their head inspected. It was mixed very strong so that nothing could live in it and had a smell similar to hot tar. The smell would stay in our hair all day. When I got home Granddad would smell the carbolic and say, 'I bet you've seen Nurse Alleygob today.' Wonder how he always knew.

Vi went upstairs to get a fine-toothed comb. The one she had just used wasn't fine enough to trap such a small insect between its teeth. When she got back, Vi had the comb and a sheet of newspaper. It wasn't a proper nit comb, but it was fine enough. There was nothing we could use to treat the fleas, so Vi planned to comb them out and kill them. The newspaper was spread flat and I held my head over it while Vi combed. It was amazing how many fleas came out onto the paper. When we thought we had got them all we got rid of the evidence in the fire, then tidied up before Auntie got back from the meeting. I was so ashamed that I didn't tell Auntie and asked Vi to keep quiet as well. The combing had relieved the itch considerably but it hadn't got rid of them all.

As soon as I got to Coombe Martin on Saturday, I told Nan about the fleas. She took me to the chemist to get some lotion. I washed my hair, soaked it with the lotion and wrapped my head with a scarf for the night. The lotion had a smell; not as strong as the carbolic, but it did get rid of the fleas. Back at work next week I often got a waft of a clinical smell coming from some of the girls. When any questions were asked the answers were vague or 'Dunno': eventually we heard the truth. A lot of the girls had been playing host to fleas as well as me.

CHAPTER 16

VE NIGHT

As we were all only very young and thought about living life to the full we were never interested in the news on the radio and our Auntie never had a morning paper. We were thrilled to bits when we arrived home from work one day to find that the war in Europe was over. We had heard on and off it was getting close. As it had been on for six long years, hearing that it was really over was very dramatic for us girls. Firstly, our boyfriends would be coming home and all the children who had been evacuated would be reunited with their mums and dads again. Some of those children had been away to safe areas from the bombing right from the beginning of the war; in some cases, not having seen their father for the full six years. If their mothers were working in a factory making munitions, these children would scarcely know their mother either, because they wouldn't get much time off from their work to go into the country areas to visit their children.

How very sad it all was: nobody would know much about each other and they would have to start being a family again. In some cases they didn't know where to begin. It wasn't only the children going home after all those years, there was their Aunties and Pops who had looked after them for the duration of the war that also mattered. Try to imagine, if you can, how they must have felt, losing their little ones as they usually called them, perhaps never ever seeing them again. I suppose a lot of them didn't. There would always be those, after going back to the big cities, would eventually go back to the country where they would have felt more secure and more loved by their Aunties and Pops.

That day was known as VE Day and the whole free world celebrated. On VE Night, as it was called, everyone in the village was so happy we kissed everyone in sight. It's a good job I didn't catch up with Robert. As many lights were turned on as they could find, but we still had to light up our candle in our bedroom to wash. When we were all dressed up, all the girls decided to walk to the Station Hotel a couple of miles up the road. Of course we didn't have very much money as usual, so we were on the cider trail again, accepting as many free drinks as we were offered. The old piano was pumping out all the old wartime songs, we were all laughing and crying at the same time. Oh what a night it was. We were able to stay until 'Last Drinks please'. It wasn't till we were on our way home, when I heard 'Johnny Zero, Johnny Zero'. Now that was the first time that I had heard our distress call. Even we land girls had our own rules and ethics and, whenever one of us needed any help at any time, Johnny Zero was the SOS call. We rallied round and saved one of the girls from an over-amorous service man.

When we got back to the village we saw the girls back to their billets, stood them up by their front doors and ran away. I didn't realize that Vi was giggling more than usual, so when we were near our cottage, I told her to be quiet when we got home. We crept in hoping Auntie wouldn't hear from the living room and started going up the stairs. Halfway up Vi started to giggle. Auntie then came upstairs and asked what was wrong with Vi. I said we felt so happy that the war was over. 'All right, my girlies, I'll speak to you in the morning.' I was glad when Vi eventually got to sleep as Auntie Lil's bedroom was next to ours and she had to walk through ours first.

After breakfast, before we went off to work, Auntie looked very serious and said, 'I thought I had always told you girlies to behave yourselves.' We both looked at her and said, 'We have, Auntie, we would never let you down,' and gave her a great big kiss.

Spring and early summer is a beautiful time to enjoy the English countryside and this year was no exception, in fact May of 1945 was a wonderful month for the people of the free world. The fighting in Europe had stopped and although there was a terrible amount of rebuilding to do we all tried to get back to normal. The weather also seemed so much better in the month of May: a good time to enjoy the beautiful scenery. All of these thoughts were in our mind as we planned a picnic for Sunday. There was a delightful spot within walking distance of the Clock Tower where we had been before. We wanted to show our appreciation to the Norwegian airmen for inviting us to their dances, so we included them in our plans. They happily accepted the invitations, so we got busy with the arrangements. There would only be a small group of us and a similar number of them. With the help of our Aunties we prepared and packed up the food, tactfully suggesting that no Slingers were required, and that we would have sweet pastries and cakes instead.

We girls made the sandwiches and flasks of tea. It was a beautiful day with the sun shining brightly which enabled us to wear light summer clothes. The boys were glad to get out of their uniforms and wear casual clothes, and we were all surprised at how young they all looked. I suppose we looked young to them too, but we were all old enough to help with the war effort.

When we arrived at the spot that we had selected, we found that we had the place to ourselves. We spread out our picnic on the grass, which was shaded by a large elm tree, and settled down to talk. Some preferred to sit out of the shade on the grass in the sun, but we were still in a group. There wasn't really a lot to do but eat and talk, but it was amazing how much we found to talk about. All of the Norwegian airmen spoke English, but we had a few laughs as they stumbled on the occasional word at times. When we were unable to make them understand we spoke with our hands, which is always a good International language, but these signs were totally different to those used in the conversation with the Ities.

What a lovely day it was because they were looking forward to going home to Norway. Some of them had been in England a long time and hadn't been able to go home on leave as we had done. We all exchanged addresses and said that we would visit them on holiday. We weren't able to give a phone number as very few working-class people had a phone at that time. Little did we realize how difficult life was to be after the war:

travel and holidays were right out of the question. As we packed up to go home, the boys thanked us for a lovely day. We had all enjoyed ourselves, talking and eating out of doors in the beautiful countryside, so different for them away from routine and discipline and us away from heavy work. The simple pleasures are always much more enjoyable, aren't they?

Sunday afternoon, Rose, Pauline and I decided to hire a bike and cycle to Winkleigh, seven miles away. The bikes looked a bit ancient, but they had two wheels and that's all we needed. Although it was spring and very cold, we enjoyed the exercise and soon warmed up. There were a few hills on the way, but mostly going up, so we knew it would be easy downhill going home.

When we arrived at the Airforce camp they knew who we were and let us in. We stayed for afternoon tea and listened to some records of Vera Lynn, who was very popular. They called her the Forces' Sweetheart. Most of her songs were rather sad because they were more for the boys who were serving overseas. Then we bade them farewell and off we went.

It was good for most of the time, but when we came to one of the steep hills, Pauline and Rose took off in front of me. As I was going down the hill I realized I was going too fast for my liking, but when I put my hand on the brake nothing happened. I got the wind up then, so I had to think fast. Just ahead of me I could see a farm gate ajar and thought, 'Right, that's where I'll head for,' which I did, not realizing that the field had been recently ploughed. Can you imagine what was happening to me? It was surprising how far the bike kept going with me hanging on like grim death. Eventually, off I came in no ladylike manner with the bike on top of me. After gathering my senses I knew I couldn't move. I must have lain there for a good half-hour when I heard the girls bellowing, 'What the hell are you doing there?' They wouldn't believe I couldn't move, and stood there laughing.

After a while it sank in and they helped me onto the bike, with a lot of moaning and groaning coming from me. I was in such a lot of pain, but knew we had to get home before it got dark. Don't ask me how I got back in the village, where Auntie said I must go straight to bed. I didn't put up a fight because I was glad to get there.

Auntie brought up a hot-water bottle which took a lot of the pain away. Strange though it may seem, no one ever took pills in those days: it was rest I needed, so my Auntie Lil said. I stayed in bed for a couple of days. It was murder having to get up to go to the toilet, especially walking up and down the stairs. On the third day Vi came and said that I had to have a certificate from the doctor for her to take back to work with her in the morning. How I managed to get up and have a wash down, yes still in icy cold water, and get up the hill to see the doctor, I never knew. I shuffled all the way, and when it was my turn to see him, a nice old country doctor, he diagnosed that I'd got lumbago. I said, 'I can't have that at my age, it's only old people who get that.' There was no tablets; I just had to rest, he said.

Each day was a little easier and I went back on the Saturday morning, and he said, 'Why have you come back so soon?' I said I was feeling much better, and asked if he would sign me off so I could go back to work on the Monday. He took one look at me and said, 'Sit down, m'dear.' I said, 'I would rather stand if you don't mind.' He had a certain grin on his lovely old face and said, 'Oh there's a dance at the Town Hall tonight, isn't there, and you don't want to miss it, do you?' I knew that if he didn't sign me off I wouldn't be able to go to the dance. In those days you were not supposed to go out if you were not signed off. I nodded and just waited to hear what he had to say. 'No, my dear, you need much more rest before you can go back to work.' Of course I didn't like what he said, but later knew he was right. I suffered for a long time and had to be careful before lifting anything heavy.

During the first few months after the crash on the bike, I began to become aware of my back injury. Thank goodness we weren't doing any heavy work like picking up potatoes and lifting the full sacks. I avoided going to the doctor because I knew he would put me on the sick list for more rest. This would also mean that I couldn't attend the dances. Remember that I was only twenty years old at the time and loved dancing. At that age I was prepared to put up with a lot of discomfort to make sure that I could be at those dances. I mean, Charlie Bissett was relying on young people like me, and I couldn't let him down, could I?

From time to time my Auntie Lil would ask, 'Are you all right, m'dear?' I would always tell her I was. She must have known that I was in pain. You see, some time after I came off the bike we were loading wheat in bags. With this kind of work, I must have strained my stomach muscles as well as my back. A full wheat bag is a heavy dead weight of about 150 pounds designed to be lifted by men with strong leg and back muscles. I suppose I was lucky that my legs were not affected. I couldn't imagine sitting it out at a dance as that was the highlight of the week. It was the time when we could wear our nice clothes and, on one of my leaves, Les my boyfriend had brought me a beautiful pair of silk stockings from America. These were as rare as hen's teeth and the other girls were so envious when I got back. All clothes were rationed and we all had clothing coupons to buy them with. These coupons were as important as money when buying clothes or shoes, and a lot of the non-essential clothes weren't available in the shops to buy. Stockings were in short supply and silk stockings were unobtainable until long after the war, so I don't have to tell you that I really treasured those stockings. I wore them for special occasions and repaired them if they got snagged. When the heels or toes wore out, I would cut a piece off the tops and sew in new ones. This took a lot of time and patience, much more than I have today, but those stockings were almost unique and I treasured them.

During the war, the American servicemen would bring stockings over to give away as presents; however, this would only be when they first came, because once they were drafted to Europe they stayed for a very long period of time. In wartime we all had to do as we were told, but we all helped one another and were happy to be alive. It wasn't until some time after the war that stockings came back into the shops. By then they were being made from a new material called nylon. They were very expensive but clothing coupons were phased out over a period of years.

As the time went on, my back was playing me up. I didn't complain very much because young girls didn't have lumbago, did they, and I felt quite ashamed to admit it. Maybe I should have kicked up a bit more fuss. Perhaps I would have gained some sort of compensation. I wonder if they paid anyone in those days, I doubt it. We took it all in our stride.

I had written to my Nan who was back home by then as it was after the war, and told her about my back. The next letter I got from her advised me to see the welfare lady and say it might be better if I came home. I saw Mrs Phillip and she must have gone to see the doctor. A few weeks later I was on my way home. The thought of going home to all the family was lovely, but the goodbyes were awful. As I sit here writing this, I can't believe I never went back to North Tawton until 1977, and that was after 32 years.

CHAPTER 17

STARTING LIFE ANEW

A djusting to a new life back home was very strange. Jean from early childhood days was still away in the Land Army. Jobs were very hard to find after the war because all the service people from home and abroad were also looking. The services were paid when they were demobbed, but we land girls got nothing. As we girls used to say, 'We may be poor but we've got our pride.' I managed to get a few hours' work not far from where I lived. I didn't think at the time; it wasn't really the type of work a young girl of 21 should be doing. It was work, therefore I got paid, that was it. It worked out very well a few months later when I received a telegram from my boyfriend Les saying, 'How about an April wedding?' You see where we lived, you were only supposed to get married in a church within your parish. The church that I wanted to be married in was not in my parish, but was where I was working. I showed Mrs Galvin, the lady I was working for, the telegram. She knew about the church and she was delighted to help me out by using her address. So I got cracking and booked the church.

Sadly, my lovely old Granddad had died in the February. I did offer to postpone the wedding but Nan said Granddad wouldn't have wanted that. I was rather impressed with the lovely, dark-green Daimler cars which were used for my Granddad's funeral, so I did no more: I marched into the Co-op Funeral Division to book a couple for my wedding. I wonder what they really thought of me. They directed me to the right office.

In the mean time I got a job as assistant stewardess at the local golf club just up the road from where I lived, and I loved it. They were very kind to me and I worked very hard there. When they offered us the golf club to have the reception, I arranged everything myself. Les was only going to be home for two weeks, and I wrote to my friend Jean because we had always planned to be each other's bridesmaid. She couldn't make it because she was being married on the 2nd April and mine was going to be 11th April. In the end, Rose, the land girl from next door, became my bridesmaid. Everything went off very well.

In those days, of course, you couldn't buy a wedding dress. Every girl who got married did so either in a suit or a dress. If they could borrow a wedding dress they were very lucky, and I happened to be one of those lucky ones. Relations from up north, whom I had never met, sent down a dress together with the veil. Their daughter had been recently married, but you would have thought that this dress had been made to measure for me. It was a beautiful dress and I was absolutely delighted.

The morning that I was getting married I had to get up quite early and go around to the golf club to lay the table. My Nan came around with me and we set the table. My Nan and my mother provided the food. My Nan had had a lovely, three-tiered horseshoe cake made for us which looked lovely on the tables, and there were beautiful flowers, and I was so pleased. I rushed home to have a bath because I was getting married at half-past twelve. It was a wonder I turned up at the church on time because the morning went so fast. How I got ready so quickly I'll never know. My future mother-in-law had come up from Clacton on Sea in Essex. She came upstairs into the room and she didn't even say, 'How lovely you look.' She didn't need to because I knew I did.

Rose my bridesmaid was also lucky because the bridesmaid dress I had worn for my sister Joyce's wedding fitted Rose and that was a lovely mauve. My bouquet was white carnations and Rose's bouquet was anemones, so they went very well together. They each had lots of trailing ferns that came right down to the floor; that was the fashion in those days. My bouquet cost me three pounds and Rose's bouquet cost me two pounds. That was an awful lot of money in those days, but when I was ordering them I didn't even ask how much they would cost, so it was a bit of a shock when we got the bill.

1946 The Wedding of Marg and Les

After the reception we all went around to my Nan's house and I got changed into the going-away suit that I had recently bought. We got into the car and a couple of other people had cars also to take us down to see us off at the station. When we set off there was so much noise because they had tied a lot of old tin cans and boots on the back of the car and it made a terrible noise. One of the boots was my brother in-law's working boot and when we got down to the station they just lifted up all these things and stacked them on the bumper-bar at the back and came down on the station so that they could wave us off on the train. Apparently when they got back, all the tin cans were there but of course Doug's boot was missing. I suppose they should have spent all night looking for a one-legged man to see if he'd pinched his boot.

When the train stopped at Charring Cross, Les ushered me into a taxi and it stopped outside the Strand Hotel. It was a wonderful surprise; as you know the Strand was a very expensive place to stay. We could only stay there for one night then the next morning we took the train down to Hayling Island and stayed in the caravan there for about a week and a half.

We arrived home after our honeymoon at Hayling Island almost broke but extremely happy. One of our first jobs was to get all the empty beer bottles together and take them back to the off-licence. This wasn't because we were tidy people, it was to cash them in for the deposit that we had paid on them. It wasn't a lot of money, but it kept us for the next few days with the help of my Nan. After these few days, Les was packing up his gear to go back to sea again on another ship. Rose, who was also my bridesmaid, eventually married her sailor boyfriend Dennis. The four of us – Rose and Den, Les and I – became close friends even though we lived some distance apart.

I had a son in December 1947, and Rose had a daughter in January 1948. In August of 1948 Les was invalided out of the Merchant Navy with a duodenal ulcer. This was a big setback as it was his chosen career and times were very hard for us. We lived in rooms because there was no housing and, if there had been, we were desperately short of money. The people who let rooms were very selective with their tenants and didn't want young babies: we were very fortunate in having some very nice landladies where we lived.

When Tony our baby was about a year old, we managed to rent a small house. It was a little cottage in the village of St Osyth, five miles from Clacton on Sea; an end cottage in a row of four; over four hundred years old. Each cottage backed onto a small yard with a water pump shared by all the tenants. Behind that we each had a garden of our own. The cottage needed a bit of work, but it had a front door and a back door and that was all we needed.

We were only two miles from the beach and Rose and Den would often come down from London with their family. They would stay with us in the cottage and we would spend our weekends picnicking on the beach. In the evenings Rose and I would have a fabulous time talking about the good old days in the Land Army. Den and Les used to tinker with the old cars that we had and then go to bed, but Rose and I would natter away till the small hours of the night.

We had our second son in 1954, and Rose and Den had another daughter and a son during that same time. All the children got on well together and Rose's children were absolutely fascinated by the pump in the yard. Her second daughter took all her clothes off and stood under it while the others stood on the tip of toe to push the handle up and down. But when we all sat down to eat, Rose and I made sure *they all ate every scrap of potato.*

In February 1960, Les and I emigrated to Albany, Western Australia to start a new life. Albany at this time was a coastal town of some 15,000 people whose lives were dependent on primary farm production. It was the regional port of export and grain, wool, frozen meat, apples and sundry other products: an unspoilt town of great beauty with a temperature which is easy to live with. The town offered so much for us and our two sons that we could not have achieved had we stayed in England. We experienced a few problems in our new country, but these were minor by comparison to the range of opportunities that were there for the taking.

Most of my side of the family eventually came to live in Australia. The first to follow us was my Nan: it was important for her to see that we were all as happy as we sounded in the letters that we wrote her. Nan was followed by my mother who also settled in Albany. In 1974 my mother returned to England for a holiday. During her stay she visited my Auntie Lil in North Tawton. Getting established in a new country with two boys to educate was not easy in a rural community where life is controlled by the prices of wheat and wool, so it wasn't till 1977 that Les and I could afford to visit England.

When we were planning our first trip back to England after seventeen years, dozens of letters to relatives, friends and acquaintances were written. I hadn't seen or heard from my old school friend Jean since 1946: the only address I had was of the farm in Dingestowe in South Wales where she

1977 Marg and Auntie Lil (one year before she died at 93)

was in the Land Army, so I wrote there. It was very long shot after 31 years, but worth a try. What a wonderful surprise to receive a reply from Jean a couple of weeks later from the same address. You see she had married the farmer's son, Bill, and they had taken over the farm and the 600-year-old farmhouse when Bill's father had retired. It was to be a short holiday crammed with visits to relations and old friends and time seemed to go in a flash. Of course we fitted in a visit to my Land Army Auntie in Devon who was then 92. We spent a lovely day with her. She proudly showed us her new pensioner's bungalow that had been built on the land where the cottages had been. It was an extremely touching meeting, bringing back so many memories. We took her out to lunch, and I couldn't thank her enough for what she had done for me all those years before.

When we left Auntie that day, it was so difficult for me to say goodbye: Les had to admit that Auntie was every bit as wonderful as I had described her. She died the following year at the age of 93.

Les and I have been back to England four times since then. We always stay for part of the time in Rose and Den's beautiful thatched cottage in Gravesend, Kent. I have also kept in touch with little Doris and Vi who live quite close to each other in Edmonton, North London. I suppose you can guess what we all talk about, and that would explain the outbursts of laughter.

There have been many nostalgic and memorable moments during our trips back to England that I won't forget. The day we drove into the farm at Dingestowe to meet my old school friend Jean will always stick in my mind. Her reply to my letter after 31 years told me that she had three daughters, a son and several grandchildren. What I didn't know was, what was Jean like, had she changed? When we arrived she looked much the same as she had done years before. I had thought about my yearning I had for her red shoes at school and the Land Army breeches when we were teenagers, but the first thing she said was, 'Didn't I tell you, Sally, Marg has still got her own teeth.' Sally was one of Jean's daughters who was staying with her for a holiday. While I was wanting the red shoes and the breeches, Jean was envying my teeth.

CHAPTER 18

STRAND PALACE ANNIVERSARY

P lanning a holiday in Britain when you live in Australia is always exciting and the success of any trip starts with the careful attention to detail. The trip we took in April 1994 was even more exciting because I had recorded most of the material for this book, and the plan was to find and meet up with as many of the North Tawton land girls as I could. Having made several visits to Britain before, we knew the art of booking in good time on our preferred airline Cathay Pacific; to stop over for a few days in Hong Kong and then to fly non-stop for 13½ hours from Hong Kong to London; to get passports, airline tickets and the money changed for the stop-over in Hong Kong; to have money for departure tax, taxis and other expenses, before we reached our final destination, our base address with my friend Rose in Gravesend. Lots of letters were also written by Les and me to all the people we wanted to see in the various countries that we visited, making sure that it all went smoothly. Added to all the usual activity we also wrote to the *Okehampton Times* in Devon telling them about the research for the book and of the pending visit to North Tawton in June. The letter included our Perth address and the address of our base in Gravesend in Kent.

Our plans did go smoothly and we arrived at Heathrow at 6 a.m. on the 11th April on a bright, cold morning, together with four other Jumbos. This meant there were hundreds of passengers from other parts of the world trying to get the clearance through customs and immigration at the same time. It took a while for us to get through but we had time on our side, so it didn't matter much. Once through we had a cup of tea to let the crowds get away. We took the bus to Hyde Park Corner where we got a taxi. I didn't hear where Les told the driver to take us, as the noise of the jet engines still rang in my ears. It was our wedding anniversary and unknown to me Les had booked us in at the Strand Palace Hotel where we had spent our first night 48 years before. What a lovely surprise that was.

Our room wasn't ready when we arrived, so we did our banking and other business and made several phone calls, fighting off our tiredness as we went. You see, although I have flown thousands of miles all over the world I never sleep on a plane, no matter how comfortable the seats are. So by the time we got to our room all we wanted to do was to rest.

This holiday was to last five months, so we carried lots of clothes for all climates. Our total luggage consisted of three suitcases, two large flight bags plus lots of bits and pieces such as duty-free drinks and top coats for the cold weather. We had scattered all of this around the room filling every bit of space and everywhere looked cluttered up. The room wasn't very big by today's standards and we thought that the Palace had lost its old wartime splendour.

We have found that the best way to avoid jet lag is to keep awake until it is dark in the country that you arrive in, and to rest by laying flat on the bed. They say that this allows the tiredness to go out through your feet. It is, however, very restful.

I lay down flat on the bed just as I was. Les didn't want to lie down in his best trousers and didn't want the trouble of changing because it meant undoing a case. Then I suggested that he take his trousers off and put on a pair of long johns, that were brought in case it turned very cold. You know I hadn't noticed his trousers come off, the first time we were here. The long johns had been put in one of the flight bags for easy access, so he put them on for the first time. They were tight fitting and pure white. He hung up his trousers and laid flat on the bed beside me. It was by now early afternoon and we had to talk to each other to stay awake.

It was fairly quiet in the room, despite the fact that we were in the Strand, in the heart of London. We talked about all manner of things, which we have done many times before. Then the quiet was broken by a knock on the door. Les got up: he looked like a long white beanstalk as he went to open the door. Outside he saw a very tall West Indian hotel porter in smart uniform carrying a tray. On the tray was a bottle of champagne in an ice bucket, two glasses and a card conveying the compliments of the management on our wedding anniversary. Les asked the porter in. There was nowhere for him to put the tray down because of all our luggage and junk that was scattered about. I also expect that the long johns made him feel uncomfortable, so he just said, 'Oh I'll put it on the floor.' Les bent down to pick up the tray, giving the porter a rear view of the long johns as he left the room. When Les brought the tray round to show me the champagne and the card, I told him he had the long johns on back to front; the fly opening was at the back. Heaven knows what the porter thought of the rear view, but we had a good laugh and I took his photograph holding the tray while still wearing his long johns.

This incident had given us something else to talk about and helped to keep us awake, while we were resting. I wonder what story the porter told the staff downstairs.

When I spoke to Rose on the telephone she said there was a letter for us from Devon and her husband Den was back in Guy's Hospital. We weren't far from there so we went to see him that evening. He was very sick and heavily sedated. He didn't speak but he did let us know that he knew we were there.

When we returned to our hotel we had a light meal and a glass of wine before an early night in bed. We didn't feel up to celebrating so the champagne didn't get opened, and although it was our anniversary in the same first-night hotel, it was a little different the second time around.

The next morning we decided to move on to Gravesend, so Les rang through to Concierge to ask for a porter to take our luggage down to the car. When the porter came to the door it was the same big bloke that had brought up the champagne. Les was a bit embarrassed and tried to explain, while the porter put the luggage on the trolley. He gave him a tip and the porter said, 'Thank you, sir,' and swung the trolley ready to push it towards the lift, and then he said, 'Excuse me sir, I can't spend this sort of money here,' and gave the coin back to Les. It looked like a British one pound coin, but it was Hong Kong money. The porter was quickly given a one pound coin in exchange and went away apparently happy. But I bet he was thinking, what a funny lot those Australians are, it must affect them down under being upside down all the time.

Travelling so fast across the world enables us to stay in new and older hotels, many of which have been refurbished, and we are able to compare accommodation and service from place to place. The Strand Palace had been refurbished but it had lost its former splendour of the 1940s. Being an old building there are some alterations that can not be made for structural reasons. One thing that hasn't changed is the service that guests receive. Being ex-patriot English, we claim that it is the good old English service that you can't get anywhere else. But wait a minute, the girl in reception was Swiss, the man in Concierge was Austrian, the Guest Service Director was from New Zealand, the Waiter was Hungarian, and the Breakfast Chef was Spanish, and of course our porter was West Indian. I suppose the reason for such good service is that the Executive Manager is English: yes, definitely a Pom, but I didn't meet him.

With so much luggage we had to order a car to take us to Gravesend. In keeping with the service of the hotel a large black chauffeur-driven car came to pick us up. Dressed in a dark blue uniform and peaked cap, the driver loaded our luggage and opened the car doors for Les and me to get in.

Once clear of central London, we noticed that the chauffeur had an accent. 'Are you English?' I asked. 'No, Madam,' he replied, 'I'm from Italy.' That good old English service is much more cosmopolitan than I had realized. And as for the car, that was a Mercedes. Ah well, *there will always be an England.*

CHAPTER 19

RETURN TO NORTH TAWTON

The weather was sunny but cold as we drove from Greater London into Kent. 'The Garden of England', as it is called, looked fresh and green on the lovely spring day. We pulled up to the thatched cottage where Rose lives and the gardens were a mass of spring flowers, birds and bees. The movement of the car on the drive made the rabbits scamper back to the fields behind the hedgerow where there was a crop of peas growing: these must be the best-fed rabbits in Kent.

Rose was all smiles as she greeted us, but looked very tired as we had expected. Her husband Den, whom we had visited the night before, had received all kinds of treatment for cancer over the previous three and a half years. Sadly he lost the battle the day after we got to Gravesend. This meant that our role now was to console and comfort Rose and her family following their loss.

The letters that arrived for me over the next couple of weeks came as a result of the article in the *Okehampton Times*. The first was from Bill and Dorothy Stoneman on behalf of the Historical Society. They were writing the history of North Tawton In Living Memory. They had some wonderful stories of bygone days in the village. Bill had been the postman when the land girls were there. Little did they realize that our base at *Thatched Cottage*, Gravesend, was the home of Rose who was one of the twelve land girls. Rose remembered Bill as postman all those years ago.

Receiving this first letter helped Rose to take her mind off her loss and she recalled many amusing stories that occurred before I was transferred to North Tawton. Then I got two big surprises in two days. The first was a

115

lovely long letter and some photographs from Rosie Stevens (Née Spratt) from Liskeard in Cornwall. She was so excited that her pen didn't stop moving as she wrote ten pages. Rosie was one of the two Rosies that stayed on in Sampford Courtenay and both married local chaps. That night I rang Rosie and this proved to be real tonic for Rose and me as we both spoke to her for almost an hour. The next day the postman brought surprise number two, a lovely letter from Hilda, the driver of the van, from Bradford in Yorkshire. She also had relatives in North Tawton. Once again the phone rang hot that night as we spoke to Hilda. She certainly hadn't lost her sparkle of 50 years before and related some of her own experiences, mostly before I got there. Hilda said she would come to North Tawton, as she visited the village quite often.

Each day another letter seemed to come from people who were associated with the Land Army or their landladies. Don Brealey was the son of Rose's landlady and nephew to my landlady, Auntie Lil. Both Rose and I remember him from all those years ago. He enclosed a copy of the newspaper article for me to see. How the memories flooded back to those days of comradeship and the fact that we all still cared.

My second surprise was to hear from Dr Jean Shields, who was the daughter of Mrs Phillip, our welfare officer. Dr Jean was only a young schoolgirl when we were in the village. She went on to train and qualify to become the local doctor. As a child she recalls visiting the girls at work and in the fields and at the homes in their billets. It was her mother, Mrs Phillip, that went to great lengths to see that we were happily settled and well cared for. I wonder if she really knew how well my Auntie Lil looked after Vi and me. There were also a number of letters from people in North Tawton and from the surrounding towns and villages that were related to the landladies of other girls, together with letters from other people who were associated with the land girls in other ways, such as children of the farmers at that time. There was a very touching letter from Mrs Bridgeman, now living in Crediton, who was the young wife of a farmer when the land girls were in town. I later learned that she is 90 years old but would still like to read my story.

A quick recap told me I was now in touch with five of the girls and that Rose and Hilda knew the address of Pauline in Middlesborough. I also knew that Nobby and the other Rose from Sampford Courtenay had died. No one had kept in touch with Joan (originally from London), Brenda (whose bridesmaids wore wellies) and Birdie (who came from the North of England), but with seven of us in all and so many associated and interested people it was essential that we all get together.

Les is good at correspondence and organizing events so I appointed him Honorary Secretary at a salary that I could afford . . . *free.* A phone call to Dorothy and Bill Stoneman put him in touch with the local pub, *The Ring of Bells.* Les booked the reception room above the pub and food for the evening of Saturday 4th June. This date suited most people, but there were still those that couldn't come: little Doris whose husband was unwell, Vi who was looking after her grandchildren, and Pauline who was on holiday in Spain. However, it was wonderful to hear Rose say that she would come with her daughter Denise.

A week before the get-together Les and I set off for the West Country. We stayed overnight at Milton Hall, Salisbury, a lovely hotel that was managed extremely well. We continued our journey next day heading for Okehampton in Devon. As we entered the town we saw a sign which said 'Motel'. We have lots of motels in Australia but they are very rare in England. I went in and looked at the room while Les sat in the car. The accommodation didn't impress me after the comfort of the hotel the previous night, so I had to say something to get out. I simply told the girl that my husband was in a bad mood because the place we stayed at last night was uncomfortable and he didn't sleep. Not true of course, but it was all I could think of at the time. The young girl was undaunted and said, 'I've got a room with twin beds if you've had a barney with your husband,' but we didn't accept her offer and went to the *White Hart Hotel.*

At lunchtime we found a lovely little place in the museum, where all the food was home cooked. Neither of us was very hungry, so we decided on a ploughman's lunch. This is usually bread, cheese and pickles, but the menu also listed ham, chicken and prawns in place of cheese. Les loves fish providing that it is fresh. When the young waitress came, he said to her, 'What are the prawns like?' meaning, 'Are they fresh?' But in a broad Devon accent, the girl said, 'They are little pink wurly things.' Oh, aren't they such funny people?

We occupied our time making arrangements for Saturday evening; meeting some of the people that had written and organizing the food, the press and the photographers. We visited the office of the *Okehampton Times* and the *Credited Courier* and were given a very good reception at each office. Both papers later published stories and photographs of the land girls as they were then and now.

Rose and her daughter Denise were due to arrive at Copplestone Station at 4.15 p.m. This was the nearest request stop to North Tawton. We set off an hour before expecting to be at least half an hour early to meet the train. The station is a platform by a single track with little else. It is also unmanned and very bare of essentials, with no shelter and an appearance of being miles from civilization: a very cold appearance. The day was also cold with frequent light rain showers on the windscreen. We drove along the winding country road and turned into the station approach road. To our complete surprise, Rose and Denise were sitting on their cases at the side of the road; cold, wet and feeling miserable. There was no sign of life around the station; not a soul in sight, no telephone, no taxi, no cars and they had been there for about half an hour. We had been given the wrong timetable information.

Back at the hotel, they freshened up and we had a long chat before dinner, then we prepared to meet Hilda at the *White Hart* pub at the bottom of the hill. It must have been 9 p.m. before Hilda arrived (way past our bedtime). Then, with a flourish like a music hall artist, Hilda entered. Her copper-coloured hair had now changed to silver but she was really alive and active. Its hard to describe the nostalgic feeling experienced by Rose and me, meeting an ex-land girl after 50 years. It was a wonderful feeling of comradeship as the memories came flooding back. We talked and laughed as we recalled and remembered so many things that happened all those years ago. It is lovely to think that Rose, Hilda and I could laugh at our experiences of 50 years before, yet we could feel the closeness of belonging.

It was pretty late when we drove back to Kayden House, our private hotel, after a long, busy day.

CHAPTER 20

GETTING TOGETHER

We were up early next morning, despite the late night and we all met as planned for morning tea. Hilda was still in high spirits and did her exercises to show how free she was from arthritis in her knees.

It was Saturday and we all looked forward to the get-together that night at 6.30 p.m. However, the morning belonged to the main street and the shops. Although there aren't many shops in the main street of North Tawton, they are always interesting to look at. It's also an ideal situation in which to meet the local people.

Rose and Hilda had gone to the Post Office, while Denise, Les and I went to the General Store a few doors away. The main shop was not very big but part of it went back a long way in an L shape. It was full of every conceivable stock item you could think of: haberdashery, stationery, toys, plastic, kitchenware, clothes, shoes . . . Well you name it, they stock it. It was such an interesting shop and it was full of people.

After we had browsed around, the three of us were making our way out to meet with Rose and Hilda. The people near the counter moved to let us through. A lady had just asked for a zip fastener and the shopkeeper bent down behind the counter to find the zip. Just as we were passing the counter a customer shouted over the heads of everyone, 'Have you got any of that knicker elastic?'

'We've got plenty of that,' the voice behind the counter said.

'Three and a half inches,' as she held up a zip. I looked at Denise and Les and none of us could contain our laughter. It was so funny that the tears rolled down our faces; to hear that deep, rich Devon accent shouting out that her unmentionables needed replacement support. Heaven knows what all the people in the street outside thought when the three of us came out crying with laughter, and attempting to repeat that request for knicker elastic. Of course we did not know who that customer was until some time later, but she is one of the locals we won't forget. It was the story of the day; we laughed each time it was told. Our rich Devon accents improved no end that day.

After lunch we took it easy and got ready for the evening. We had to arrive early and the excitement mounted as we walked down the little street to *The Ring of Bells*. It was ten minutes to six as we climbed the stairs to the room above. When we turned into the room a lady stood up and with a huge smile said 'Hello'. Rose and I exclaimed at the same time, 'Rosie Spratt.' Our last meeting had been in 1945 and the feeling of excitement that hit our stomachs and our throats is hard to describe.

For a while this excitement completely clouded out the efforts put in by the publican, Norm Parish, his family and team. The room was set out with individual tables for six around the sides. Flags and decorations hung from the ceiling with a Union Jack on one wall. Coloured lights lit different areas and small flashing fairy lights helped create a warm atmosphere. All this was enhanced by the little cocktail bar in the corner and the background music of the 1940s.

We three land girls were talking at twenty to the dozen, our chatter only being broken as we met the other guests as they arrived. It seemed at first as if only a few people were going to turn up, but this proved to be wrong. We had set the starting time at 6.30 p.m., which was a bit early for the local people. It was also a cold wet night that could have slowed the people down. This quiet start only lasted until more and more guests turned up and Hilda made another gushing entrance.

What precious moments they were to meet Don and Audrey Brealey after all these years, to renew the acquaintance of Bill Stoneman, the postman, and his wife Dorothy from the Historical Society, and what a pleasant surprise when Jack and Kennedy Gregory came to renew old acquaintances. Jack now runs a very successful trucking company in North Tawton. All four of us land girls felt a special empathy with Doctor

Jean Shields, the daughter of our Welfare Officer, Mrs Phillip. She had made a special effort to come from an earlier engagement in Exeter. There were also twenty or more other people from the District, each having a particular story to contribute to the wonderful evening.

The reporter from the local paper took notes for the newspaper article and the photographer took pictures of the girls that were also published. With the photographs out of the way, supper was served. This consisted of hot and cold buffet-style finger foods which were beautifully prepared and presented on a large table to one side.

Coming from Australia, Les and I noticed how shy the English country people were, as no one wanted to be first to pick up a plate and choose their supper. From the time each group had arrived they had remained together in their own little party at one of the tables.

We had been used to circulating among all the guests because we had plenty of practice on previous occasions in Australia. You see, when we were younger, Les was a Councillor on the Albany Town Council and it was part of our Civic duties to circulate among visitors to our town at Civic Receptions and other public functions. We continued this practice in our own business as we made a point of talking to the customers at each table in our Steak House. This wasn't always easy as the restaurant seated 150 people and there were plenty of very busy nights, but the customers always liked to be able to say that the owners came to talk to them.

So we moved around the people at *The Ring of Bells* that evening. At one table Les told Bill and Dorothy Stoneman about the incident in the General Store that morning, and he put on a real Devon accent as he said 'knicker elastic'. Not many of the others heard the story. Les moved on once he had got them laughing. Some time later he returned to that table and Dorothy said, 'I've told them about the knicker elastic.' She had a huge grin on her face as one of the ladies up the other end said, 'That were I.' . . . Oh dear! So what did Les do? He just smiled and promised her a place in the next book.

The evening was very informal as it wasn't an occasion for speeches. Everyone was happy to talk and to eat and later even dance on the centre of the floor that had been left clear. This pattern was only broken by Hilda who gave a vote of thanks to Les and me for organizing this evening. She then presented me with a lovely still-art tray, which represented the work of the land girls. Mounted on a basket work tray, Hilda had arranged an array of various miniature hand-baked loaves of bread and rolls; this was decorated with ears of corn and blackberries, giving a real harvest festival effect to the display. The plaque now hangs on the wall in the room where we first planned the meeting of the land girls, in Perth Australia. Below it is a commemorative plate which tells how it was presented by Hilda at the get-together in North Tawton.

Saturday night in a country pub is where the locals find their entertainment and varying activities. Going on below where the get-together was held, the usual activities for Saturday night were taking place. There was a country and western singer with guitar and drum machine, dancing, sing-along, as well as a 21st-birthday party group. Other activities included draughts, darts and of course drinking, in an atmosphere that can only be experienced in an English pub.

Our party was thinning out at about 10.30 p.m., so the remaining dozen or so of us decided to relocate at a large table in the main bar. There had been quite a lot of food not eaten, so we asked Donald to put it on the table where the 21st celebration was being held. The young people soon showed their appreciation by eating heartily, but, as I have said previously, the food was delicious.

As we looked around all the happy people, we noticed there were the young, some with children, and the not so young, who were less active. The noise increased as the night warmed up. Voices were raised, singing got louder and the guitar and drum machine got advanced to a greater volume. In fact, the whole place seemed to be rocking. Then a couple of older men came over to ask for the land girls and one said, 'Remember us?' We looked and we all said, 'No.' Their faces dropped. Over the years they had probably got free drinks by telling the story that they had been boyfriends of the land girls. Oh well, we can all dream, can't we?

After saying goodnight to everyone, we were pleased to get back to the hotel and into bed. It had certainly been a long but very memorable day. I had even remembered to ask the other land girls if they would come to London to meet the rest of the girls that couldn't come that night. They all eagerly said that they would. As we said our farewells we knew that there was more to look forward to.

Next morning, Les and I took Rose and Denise to the Exeter station to catch the London-bound train. We had got the right timetable information this time and a train came in on time for them to board. We were spending a few more days in the West Country before our planned return to Kent.

I felt a little sad as we drove out of North Tawton but the feeling didn't last long as I had spotted a road sign which indicated a place called Whimple. This was the village where I had been sent to become a milkmaid. We drove down the street and found the pub, the shop and the station in that order. I couldn't find anyone who remembered the training dairy farm. The people I asked were too young to remember. One young girl said she would call the boss because he was born in Whimple and he was older than her. When he came from the back of the shop he looked like a typical Australian in his dark blue singlet, shorts and thongs and even said, 'G'day.' He was about the same age as my youngest son, Peter, and was eager to help. I briefly outlined that I had come from Perth and was looking for a dairy farm that I was at during the war. He was also a bit too young to remember it, but he told me that he had emigrated to Perth when he was two years old and had come back to Devon eighteen months ago to see if he would like to live there.

Now this was a real coincidence, but as we talked I realized what a small world we live in. Not only did he live in the same city as my family and me, he also knew both of our sons because of their music. He had followed the Dean Brothers Band years ago and had followed the Jets right up until he came to England. The Jets is a very successful rock band which had been formed and run for thirteen years by my youngest son, Peter. Tony, our eldest son, formed the Beatnicks, a Beatles impersonation group, which still performs out of Sydney where he and his family have settled.

The surprise at this chance meeting took away the curiosity to see the dairy farm, so I never did establish the locality of the big house where I was billeted or the cow shed where we tried to catch the dung on the shovel.

CHAPTER 21

THE REUNION

By the end of June we were near Tonbridge in Kent. I had been in touch with Rose, Little Doris, Vi, Hilda and Rose by phone and letter, to get their thoughts on a reunion in London. Hilda had also been in contact with Pauline, who was very keen to come. Any meeting that I could attend would have to fit in with holiday plans that Les and I had made before leaving Perth. Once again, Les was appointed Secretary on the same salary-free conditions. He didn't take long to establish that the 21st July suited everyone, it also avoided the weekly strikes by signalmen on British Rail that stopped most of the trains from running on Wednesdays.

The *George Hotel* restaurant was booked for midday and all the girls were informed that it was close to the railway station in Enfield, north of London.

After each of our trips to parts of Britain, Les and I would return to Rose at Gravesend for a few days. From there we would fit in visits to all manner of people and places of interest. There were still a few weeks to go before the planned reunion on the 21st of July.

It was now the 6th July, Rose's birthday, and I discovered that she would like to go to a little bookshop in Blackheath Village in south-east London for her birthday treat. We set off with the intention of browsing around the books and then having a nice lunch somewhere. The little bookshop turned out to be a display of 1920s-1950s household and other items by the Age Exchange Society. This included many items used during World War Two by housewives, air-raid wardens, firefighters, and rescue and ambulance personnel. The centre piece of the display was a fully stocked shop of the 1930s–1940s era complete with overhead invoice, money and change conveyor, propelled by a spring-loaded handle. It connected the shop assistant with the cash desk. Washing day of years ago was depicted by a galvanized bath, sunlight soap, starch, soda, scrubbing board, copper stick and a huge mangle. On the old coal stove was a flat iron to press clothes with. There were thousands of items of memorabilia collected, cleaned and restored by the society. These were shown, described and discussed by their members for the public. Groups of schoolchildren were instructed on the way life used to be by the expert lecturers using the displayed items. In all a very fascinating and absorbing idea.

And what about the books? The members had carefully collected and recorded the recollections of the older people in the district about their lives in those days. These memoirs were grouped together and printed in books that were on sale to the public. Unfortunately, we could not take everything in, in a four-hour visit. We did buy a number of their books which will keep us engrossed for hours.

On another occasion we took Rose to visit Shrewsbury House, the mansion where I had lived with my grandparents. This is where my grandfather had been appointed as caretaker for a couple of weeks and had stayed for ten years. During World War Two the house had been an Air Raid Control Centre for the Borough of Woolwich, and this is where I first met my husband, Les. The house is currently used as a community centre, housing dozens of activities on its three floors and in the grounds. It was particularly touching for me as the present caretaker took us on a tour of the house, unlocking doors as we went. The oak panelling and polished floors were still there, although they were showing signs of age. I wondered what my Granddad would think if he saw it now. Pre-war the floors and oak staircase would shine like a mirror after the polishing done by the hands of my Nan and Granddad. It was a very nostalgic visit that linked so many events and people that I have experienced during my early life.

Some days later Les and I stopped on Shooters Hill on the corner of Shrewsbury Lane. A quarter of a mile down the road was the Grotto, the house where I had been working before I was to get married. The owner had given me permission to use that address as my own so that I could get married in the little church on Shooters Hill. I walked down to see where the house was and Les followed in the car and of course I found it. The next-door neighbour, who was painting his gate, confirmed that it was the house. The Grotto was still in the front garden, overgrown by ivy. 'Should I knock at the door and ask if I could take a photo of the Grotto?' I pondered. So I did. To my very great surprise the elderly lady that owned the house was Mrs Galvin, yes, the same lady whom I had done housework for in 1946.

July was very warm and we kept ourselves busy as usual. We had made our plans to get to the reunion well in advance, so that there were no hold-ups and we would arrive there on time.

It was now the morning of the 21st and Les and I were awake early. Rose had been up for some time; she seemed to wake up as soon as it got light in the morning, just like the birds. There was plenty of time to get breakfast, get washed and dressed and out to the bus stop by nine-thirty. The bus took us to Gravesend station, where we caught the train to Charing Cross in London. Once there, we descended to the seemingly endless tunnels of the London Underground, where the tube train took us to Liverpool Street station. It was at this station that we caught the train to Enfield. From Gravesend to Enfield is a long and tiring journey by public transport and the problems were added to by the hot, humid day. We had plenty of time to notice how poor the ventilation is on tubes and trains, but I could feel the excitement building as we got closer to our destination.

Once there we quickly made our way out of the station, round to the left and across the road to where we could see the sign of the *George Hotel*. It was just after midday: a clear blue sky, the sun bearing down with a shade temperature of over 80 degrees. As we came closer to the hotel I could see a group of people sitting at one of the tables outside and recognized Little Doris and Vi straight away. There were big smiles as they all stood up and a tall, slim woman with glasses came and put her arms around me and just said, 'Marg, its lovely to see you again.' It was then that I realized that it

The Reunion: July 1994

Rose, Marg, Rosie, Hilda, Little Doris, Norma (friend), Vi, Pauline, Mick (friend)

was my Land Army friend Pauline who had come down from Middlesborough to be with us. It was hugs and kisses all round as we all said how well everyone looked. Greetings were broken by one of the girls saying, 'I'm hungry, let's eat.' But we were waiting for Hilda.

We didn't have to wait long as a voice from out of one of the large upstairs windows, shouted, 'I'm up here, you're all late.' We all went in and upstairs to the restaurant. Les had ordered one round table for eight right in the window. There were seven of us land girls and Norma, a neighbour and good friend of Little Doris. Norma and her husband Mick had brought Vi and little Doris by car to Enfield. Les and I already knew Mick and Norma because we had met and spent a lovely day with them in Fremantle and Perth. They had come in on a cruise ship several years before and we had had a wonderful day together with our friends in Perth.

A separate table out of earshot of our conversation had been booked for husbands, sons and male partners. As only Mick and Les had come they had lunch together, leaving us girls to our reunion. We all talked about our children, grandchildren and some had great-grandchildren, and lots of photographs were passed around. It was very interesting to hear a little of how different each of our lives had been since we left the Land Army. It didn't seem that it had been 50 years, now that we were all sitting at the one table together. It was such a pity that Joan, Birdie and Brenda couldn't be located to make the gang complete. From time to time during our lunch, one of the girls would say, 'do you remember this', or, 'I wonder what happened to so and so?' Usually the response would bring a burst of laughter as the most unlikely outcome was suggested.

It was all so wonderful, time seemed to pass so quickly. We talked, listened, joked and laughed just as we used to in the old baker's van back in North Tawton. One of them asked why my hair wasn't grey, and another said, 'How have you managed to keep your own teeth, Marg?' I didn't have to answer as this was done for me by another of the girls, who said, 'I suppose the National Health Service is better in Australia.' As for me, I didn't know.

I was so busy enjoying their company again after so long that I can hardly remember what I had for lunch, and I doubt if the others could either, but we did all agree later that the food was beautiful. But for all the wide range of subjects that we talked about, not one of us mentioned that we had any aches or pains from arthritis, or other old people's complaints. Nor did we talk about pills, or medication, doctors or hospital. Perhaps the hard work and country air we breathed in our younger days kept us going instead.

After we had eaten our lunch we sang Happy Birthday and gave cards and presents to Rosie from Liskeard. She was taken by surprise by this because she hadn't realized that the girls knew. So she was celebrating her birthday and a reunion at the same time and said that she would never forget this day.

The lunch had taken us three hours and the restaurant management must have been caught up with our nostalgia because they were extremely tolerant and made no hint that we were there too long. We moved outside and grouped together by the garden in front of the hotel for photographs. These came out very well and we each have a copy as a lasting memory of our special day.

It was hugs and kisses all round as we left to make our various ways home. The journey back for Rose, Les and me took longer than it had when we came. We got caught up in the rush-hour crowds as we crossed London, arriving back at Gravesend at 7.30 p.m. Once there after a wonderful day, the glow of happiness at meeting all the girls again blotted out my tiredness. Rose and I compared notes taken at the lunch table of where to locate the other land girls. We had all exchanged addresses and vowed to keep in touch with each other at Christmas and birthdays.

This day had meant a lot to every one of us and made us feel a closeness of belonging to an 'exclusive group'. To meet again after such a long time we had renewed our lasting friendships.

ENDNOTE

A compliment to Rose, little Doris, Vi, Pauline, Nobby, Birdie, Hilda, Joan, Brenda, big Doris, Rose and Rose.

It was *us* that made the Land Army *the best years of our lives.*

Regards, Marg

This is a verse that was written in our visitor's book by a British soldier.

> To the sound of Bing Crosby and Ave Maria
> Vi and with others and songs that were dear.
> Each had a song, a memory as well
> And each song belonged to a Land Army gel.
>
> So you see I shall remember when I'm far away
> The friendships I found when I came down that day.
> A welcome by all, a smile and a tear
> Yes I'll remember, year after year.
>
> God bless you and keep you
> And be of good cheer,
> If we don't meet again the memory is dear.
> Keep smiling, chin up, let's see this job through
> And we owe one and all a good deal to you.